IMPACT
CALIFORNIA
SOCIAL STUDIES

Weekly Explorer
MAGAZINE

U.S. History
Making a New Nation

DNY59/E+/Getty Images

McGraw Hill Education

mheducation.com/preK-12

Send all inquiries to:
McGraw-Hill Education
8787 Orion Place
Columbus, OH 43240

ISBN: 978-0-07-899373-2
MHID: 0-07-899373-3

Printed in the United States of America.

1 2 3 4 5 6 7 8 9 LHN 22 21 20 19 18 17

Chapter 1

The Land and People Before Columbus

ESSENTIAL QUESTION EQ

Where and how did American Indians live before the arrival of Europeans?

Chapter 2

The Age of Exploration

EQ ESSENTIAL QUESTION **What happened when diverse cultures crossed paths?**

Chapter 3

A Changing Continent

ESSENTIAL QUESTION EQ How did European settlements impact North America?

(l)Scott Sleek/EyeEm/Getty Images, (r)Alexander Sviridov/Shutterstock.com

Chapter 4

The Road to War

ESSENTIAL QUESTION EQ

Why would a nation want to become independent?

Chapter 5

The American Revolution

What does the revolutionary era tell us about our nation today?

Chapter 6

Forming a New Government

How does the Constitution help us understand what it means to be an American?

Comstock Images/Alamy

Chapter 7

Life in the Young Republic

How were the early years of the United States transformative for the nation?

Chapter 8

The Westward Expansion

What does the westward expansion reveal about the character of our nation?

ollirg/Shutterstock.com

(l)KidStock/Blend Images/Getty Images, (c)LWA/Dann Tardif/Blend Images/Getty Images, (r)Kali Nine LLC/Getty Images

Explore!

Welcome to the Weekly Explorer Magazine!

This magazine will give you a chance to explore the world.

- There are articles, songs, stories, and poems for you to read.
- You will look closely at maps, diagrams, infographics, and other images.
- As you read, you will look for answers to an Essential Question (EQ).

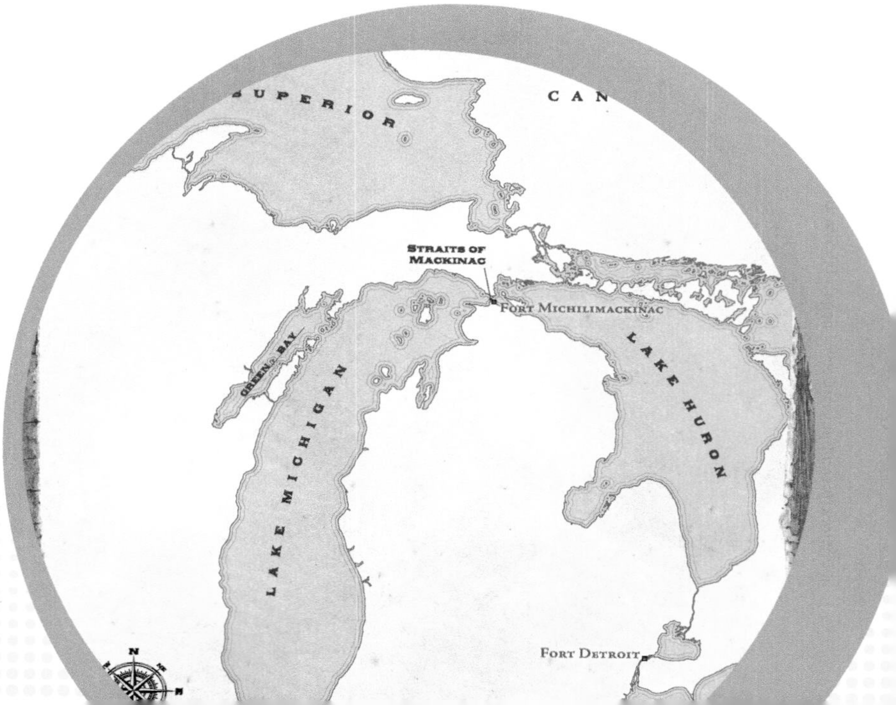

The following steps will help in your exploration.
You can take notes as you read.

1 Inspect

Read the text.

- What does it say?
- What are the details in the images?
- What are the main ideas?

2 Find Evidence

Reread the text and look at the images again.

- Look for more clues about the main ideas.
- What other details do you notice?
- How does the writer support the ideas?
- Be curious!

3 Make Connections

Think about what you've read.

- How does this connect to the EQ?
- How does it connect to other texts?
- How does it connect to you?
- What do you think?

Marc Romanelli/Blend Images LLC

Let's go!

Chapter 1

The Land and People BEFORE COLUMBUS

ESSENTIAL QUESTION EQ

Where and how did American Indians live before the arrival of Europeans?

Table of Contents

A Wise Use of Resources

This replica of a Native American hoe was made of a buffalo shoulder blade.

The Klickitat people in the Northwest used a basket like this one to gather berries.

The Paleo Indians from the Eastern Woodlands fashioned spear points from stone.

People from the Fremont culture used a metate and mano to grind corn.

- These images of tools used by early American Indian groups reflect the ways they lived. How did they use the resources around them to meet their needs?

THE UNCRACKABLE CODE

Preston Toledo and Frank Toledo were cousins who served with the Marines as Navajo code talkers.

A Land of Many Languages

When Europeans first came to North America, there were more than 300 Native American languages. The languages were spoken only; they did not include writing until after European settlement.

American Indian languages included Navajo and Apache, which were spoken in parts of New Mexico and Arizona. Paiute, Shoshoni, and Hopi were spoken in parts of Utah, Nevada, California, and Colorado. On the East Coast, Native Americans spoke languages such as Narragansett and Delaware. Some languages were in the same family, having common origins.

During World War I, an American Indian language was used creatively. Some U.S. soldiers spoke Choctaw. The United States Army used Choctaw words as a code to transmit messages. The Choctaw code helped U.S. soldiers succeed against the Germans.

The Germans and Japanese learned from this. After World War I, they sent students to study American Indian languages.

During World War II, the United States and its allies again faced a challenge. How could they send messages that could not be **intercepted**? Philip Johnston, a Marine, had grown up on a Navajo reservation. He thought the Navajo language could be used as the Choctaw language had been in World War I. Navajo was even more difficult than Choctaw. Foreign students had not studied Navajo because it was so difficult. So the Marine Corps gave twenty-nine Navajos a unique assignment: to create a code that could not be broken by the enemy.

WordBlast

What do you think **intercepted** means? How does the text help you figure that out?

The Navajos' Secret

Navajo was not a written language. It was passed down in stories, songs, and prayers. The twenty-nine original code talkers developed two codes. The Type One Code assigned a Navajo word to each letter in the alphabet. Navajo words representing letters could be put together to spell messages. In the Type Two Code, English messages were translated into Navajo. They were sent over the radio and translated into English by a Navajo speaker on the other end. The code talkers created more than 400 new words for war-related vocabulary that didn't exist in their language.

Former president George W. Bush presented the Gold Medal of Honor to Navajo code talker John Brown Jr.

The code talkers didn't just have to know the Type One and Type Two codes. They also had to learn to operate radios and set up communication lines and equipment.

The Marine Corps used the Navajo code successfully in the battle of Iwo Jima. Six Navajo code talkers sent 800 messages. All were delivered accurately.

The public didn't know about the Navajo code talkers until 1968. Today, they are considered heroes. These brave men helped the Allies win World War II.

The Tatanka and the Tribal People *of the Great Plains*

Long Live the Tatanka!

by Scott Frazier

Scott Frazier is an environmental educator and enrolled Crow tribal member. He spent his first seven years listening to his grandfather's stories. Today he lives near the Crow Reservation in Montana.

ACCORDING TO A STORY MY GRANDFATHER TOLD ME:

Long ago, the people and the Tatanka (buffalo) lived inside the world. The people cared for the Tatanka because the animals were holy. When the people came outside of the earth and were cold and hungry, the Tatanka felt sorry for them.

So, the Tatanka came outside too, to feed and care for the people. The Tatanka promised to provide everything for life on the Great Plains. The relationship between the Tatanka and the people formed a sacred oath. The Tatanka gave themselves in harvest for the good of the people.

No other animal has ever made this agreement with the people of the Great Plains. Native Americans revered their connection with the Tatanka.

And then Western civilization came to the Great Plains. By 1877, the buffalo were nearly **exterminated** in the state of Montana. The Native people were very sad at having lost their connection with the Tatanka.

With the current growth in the bison population, people are eating more buffalo, and the Tatanka are fulfilling their promise once again. Long live the Tatanka!

WordBlast

What is the meaning of **exterminated**? How does the root *terminate* help you figure out its meaning?

The Versatile Tatanka

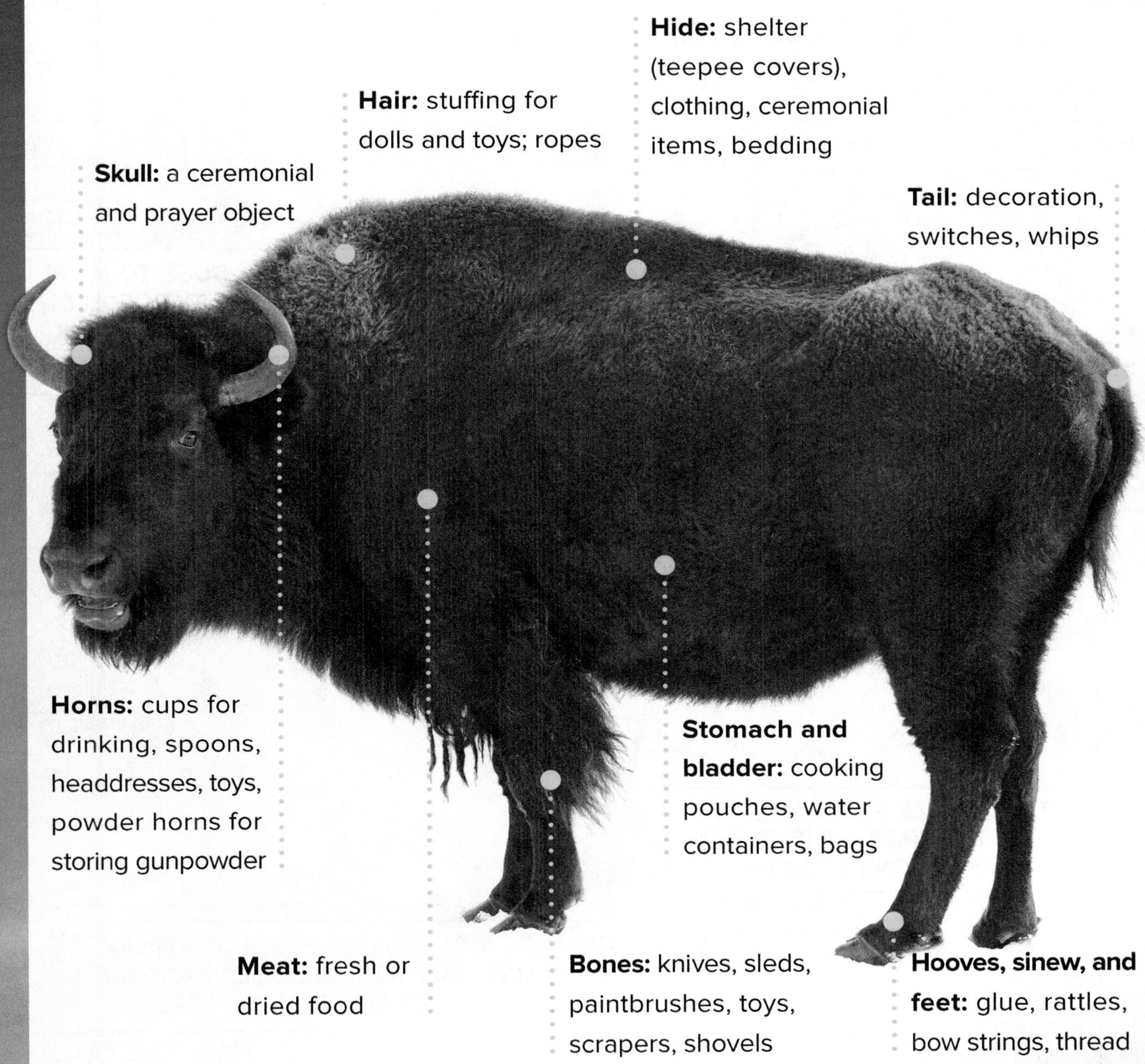

EXPLORE the Infographic

Based on the infographic, what can you tell about the lives of the people on the Great Plains?

How did the buffalo help them with different aspects of their lives?

Why do you think it was important for the Great Plains people to use nearly every part of the buffalo?

najin/E+/Getty Images

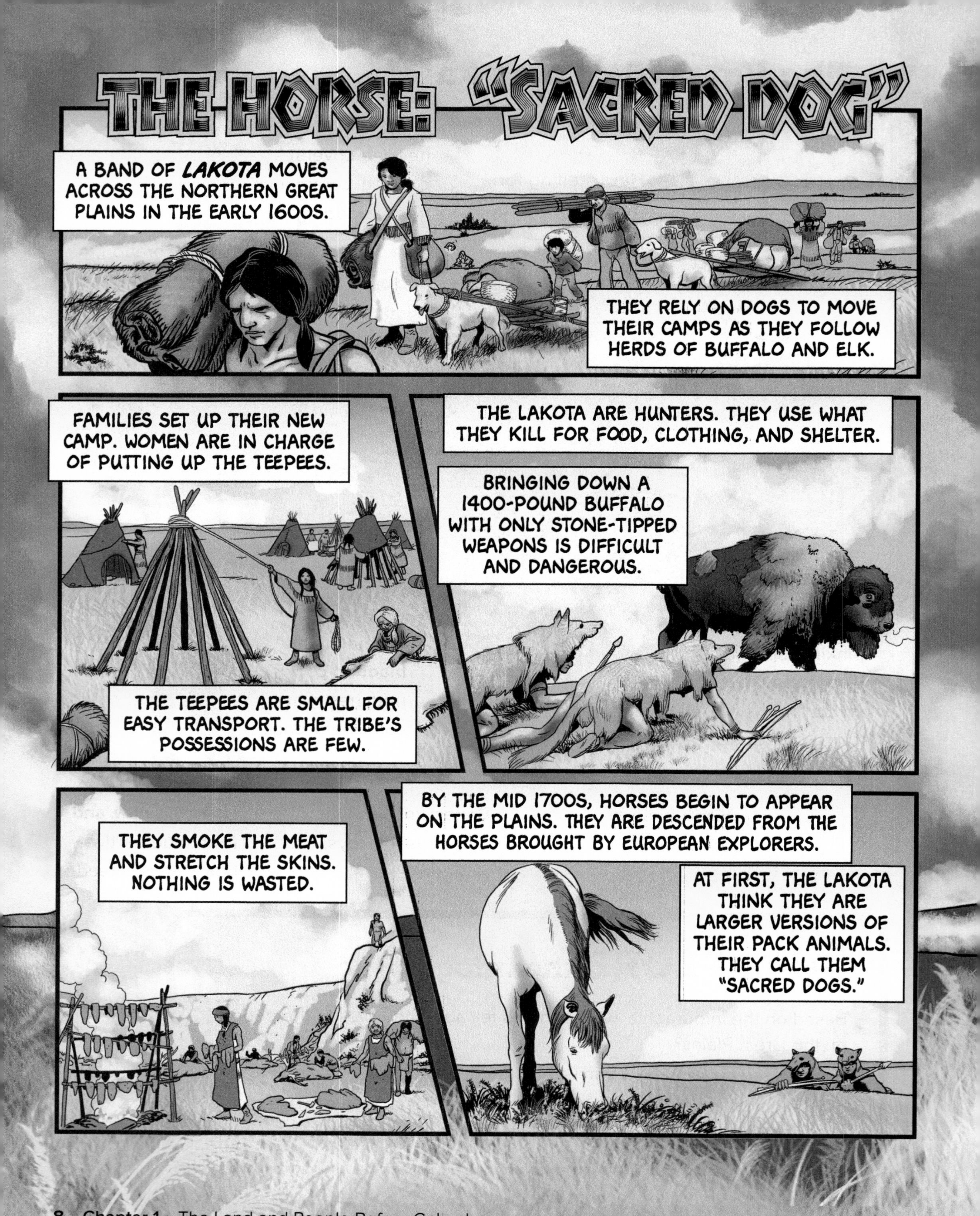
THE HORSE: "SACRED DOG"
A BAND OF *LAKOTA* MOVES ACROSS THE NORTHERN GREAT PLAINS IN THE EARLY 1600S.
THEY RELY ON DOGS TO MOVE THEIR CAMPS AS THEY FOLLOW HERDS OF BUFFALO AND ELK.
FAMILIES SET UP THEIR NEW CAMP. WOMEN ARE IN CHARGE OF PUTTING UP THE TEEPEES.
THE TEEPEES ARE SMALL FOR EASY TRANSPORT. THE TRIBE'S POSSESSIONS ARE FEW.
THE LAKOTA ARE HUNTERS. THEY USE WHAT THEY KILL FOR FOOD, CLOTHING, AND SHELTER.
BRINGING DOWN A 1400-POUND BUFFALO WITH ONLY STONE-TIPPED WEAPONS IS DIFFICULT AND DANGEROUS.
THEY SMOKE THE MEAT AND STRETCH THE SKINS. NOTHING IS WASTED.
BY THE MID 1700S, HORSES BEGIN TO APPEAR ON THE PLAINS. THEY ARE DESCENDED FROM THE HORSES BROUGHT BY EUROPEAN EXPLORERS.
AT FIRST, THE LAKOTA THINK THEY ARE LARGER VERSIONS OF THEIR PACK ANIMALS. THEY CALL THEM "SACRED DOGS."

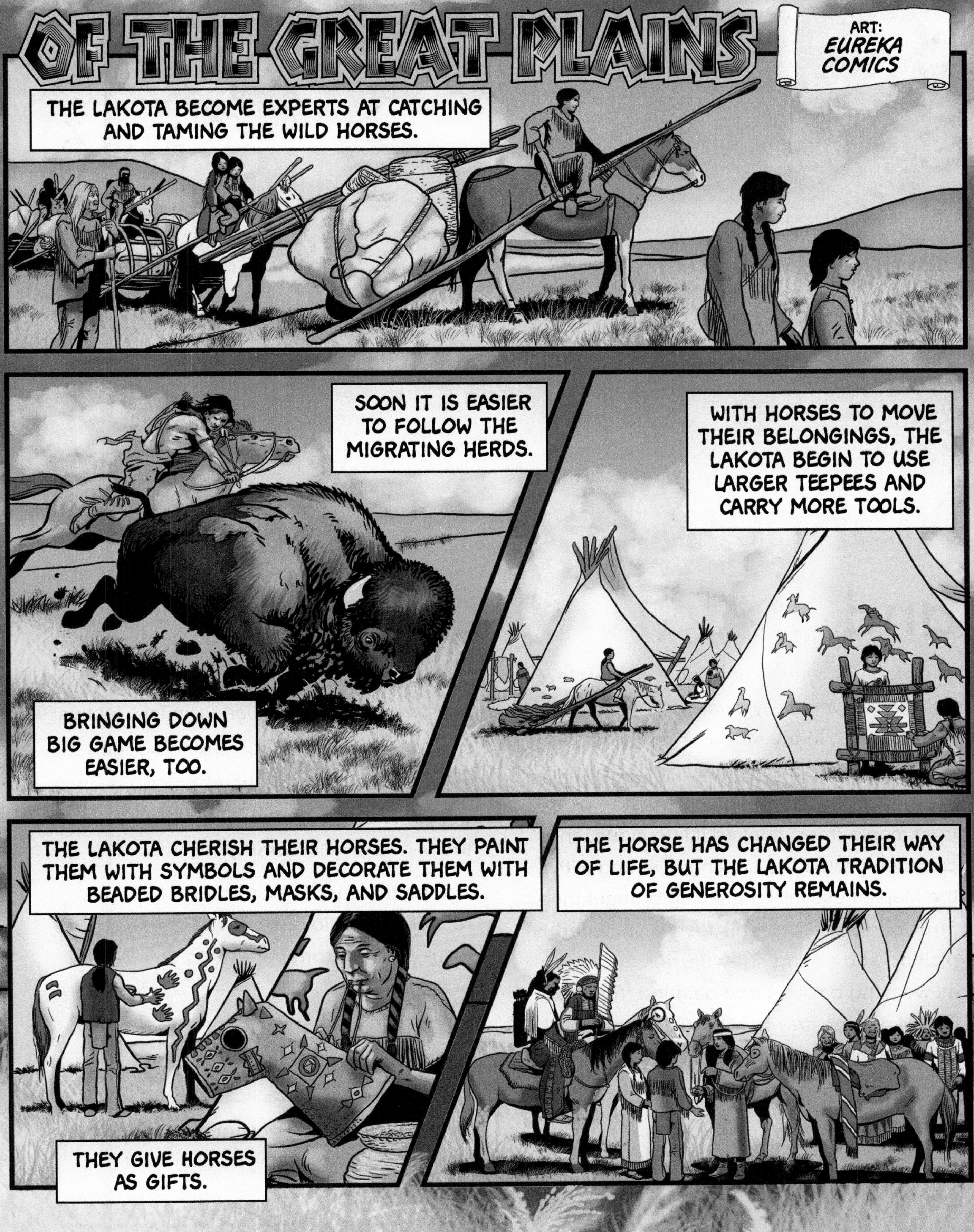

OF THE GREAT PLAINS
ART: EUREKA COMICS
THE LAKOTA BECOME EXPERTS AT CATCHING AND TAMING THE WILD HORSES.
SOON IT IS EASIER TO FOLLOW THE MIGRATING HERDS.
BRINGING DOWN BIG GAME BECOMES EASIER, TOO.
WITH HORSES TO MOVE THEIR BELONGINGS, THE LAKOTA BEGIN TO USE LARGER TEEPEES AND CARRY MORE TOOLS.
THE LAKOTA CHERISH THEIR HORSES. THEY PAINT THEM WITH SYMBOLS AND DECORATE THEM WITH BEADED BRIDLES, MASKS, AND SADDLES.
THEY GIVE HORSES AS GIFTS.
THE HORSE HAS CHANGED THEIR WAY OF LIFE, BUT THE LAKOTA TRADITION OF GENEROSITY REMAINS.

This is the article. Probably need to fact check left hand page (not easy for Native Am facts) and research write new right hand page. 2 pages.

Mohawk Feasts, Festivals, and Traditional Tales

The Mohawk, who lived in what is now New York State, were very aware of the cycle of the seasons. Many Mohawk festivals and feasts were linked to a particular time of year. In early spring, the Mohawk collected sap from maple trees, cooked it into syrup, and **commemorated** the coming of spring with the Maple Festival. Late spring brought the Strawberry Festival. This festival included picking and eating strawberries, as well as weaving baskets and painting them to look like giant strawberries. Other festivals included the springtime Thunder Ceremony and the four-day Green Corn Festival at harvest time.

The longest and most important ceremony among the Mohawk, however, was the Midwinter Ceremony. It was held every year for six to nine days in January. This festival officially ended the old year and began the new year. Babies who had been born since the Green Corn Festival were named during the Midwinter Ceremony.

The myths and legends of the Mohawk reflect their religious beliefs. These stories were passed from parents to children by oral tradition.

WordBlast

What is the meaning of **commemorated**? How does the text help you figure out the meaning of the word?

(t)Megapress/Alamy Stock Photo, (b)Marek Mnich/Getty Images

Mohawk Indians of the Northeast still perform a traditional rabbit dance similar to the dance shown here.

CONNECT THROUGH LITERATURE

A Traditional Mohawk Myth

by Carroll Moulton

One day, a group of men went out to hunt. They walked silently through the woods and stopped in front of a **clearing**, where they saw a giant rabbit. The rabbit was as big as a small bear! The leader of the hunt gave a signal to keep the hunters from shooting the rabbit. Instead they watched it carefully, sensing that something strange was happening.

The rabbit lifted its head and looked straight at the men and then stamped the ground with one foot. Other rabbits appeared in the clearing. As the big rabbit began to thump the ground, the other rabbits formed a circle and began to dance—a beautiful, complex dance. The hunters, amazed, began to tap their hands on the ground to the rhythm of the dance.

The dance ended suddenly. The rabbit chief jumped high in the air and sailed over the hunters' heads, and all the other rabbits scattered in every direction.

Back in the village, the hunters told the clan mother what they had seen. They demonstrated the dance and beat its rhythm on a drum. The clan mother then explained, "The rabbit chief has given us this dance. He knows that we depend upon the Rabbit People for food and clothing." Ever since, the Mohawk have performed the Rabbit Dance to show their appreciation for what the Rabbit People have done for them.

WordBlast

What is the meaning of **clearing**? Why is this an important detail to the myth?

Megapress/Alamy Stock Photo

Citizenship

JOSEPH BRUCHAC: *Sharing Stories*

Joseph Bruchac fascinates listeners with the stories and characters he creates.

Joseph Bruchac is a renowned storyteller, famed for his stories about animals with characteristics like people and for his engaging style. He says, "When a good story is told, it goes into a person's heart and remains there."

Listeners hearing Joseph Bruchac share a story might feel as though the world is changing around them. A flute sounds like birdsongs, breath, or wind in trees. A thumping drum feels like a heartbeat. Many of the stories Bruchac shares relate to the traditions of his Native American heritage. (His grandfather was Abenaki Indian, native to the northeastern United States and southeastern Canada.) Bruchac learned about storytelling from workmen visiting his grandfather's store.

Listeners often see themselves or someone they know in Bruchac's animal characters, such as a turtle who talks too much. Bruchac changes the sound of his voice for each character, whether human or animal. He might make a low growl for a bear or a high squeak for a mouse. Bruchac describes the storytelling process as a circle with four connected parts: *listening*, *observing*, *remembering*, and *sharing*. He believes that stories are a "living presence" that can become part of us. Bruchac hopes his stories will give listeners a deeper understanding of how all life on Earth—plants, animals, and people—is linked, as well as the importance of treating each other with respect.

Take Action!

More to Explore

Research and discuss the following questions to think about how Native American life and traditions have affected our country and culture.

What can the work of the Navajo Code Talkers in World War II teach Americans today?

What can people today learn about resourcefulness from the story of the Tatanka?

In addition to storytellers, who else passes on the traditions of a culture or people? How do they share those traditions?

WordBlast

- Would you rather live in a **clearing** or in a forest? Why?
- What are some important events that we **commemorate** each year?
- What do you think caused the buffalo to almost be **exterminated**?
- What might have happened if the enemy had **intercepted** the messages sent by the Navajo code talkers?

ESSENTIAL EQ QUESTION

Reflect

Where and how did American Indians live before the arrival of Europeans?

Chapter 2

The Age of Exploration

ESSENTIAL QUESTION EQ

What happened when diverse cultures crossed paths?

Table of Contents

Monuments and Memories

The ***Padrão dos Descobrimentos*** (Discoveries Monument) in Lisbon, Portugal, celebrates the role of Portugal during the Age of Exploration.

The ***Monumento al Cacique Mabodamaca*** (Monument to Cacique Mabodamaca) is in Isabela, Puerto Rico. This monument celebrates the brave Taíno leader Mabodamaca, who fought against Spanish soldiers in Puerto Rico in the early 1500s.

This monument in Bariay, Cuba, represents the culture of both the Spanish explorers and the Taíno people in the Caribbean.

- These three modern monuments reflect upon the period in history when European explorers encountered the native peoples of the Americas.
- What details do you notice about each monument? What mood does each monument express?

Why Did They Go?

Power! Gold!

Before Columbus began the first of his voyages, he worked out a contract with the King and Queen of Spain. The agreement said that Columbus would be "Viceroy and Governor General" of the lands he found. It also said that he could keep one-tenth of all of the jewels, gold, silver, and spices that he brought back to Spain. Exploration could make him rich!

In a later letter to the King and Queen of Spain, Columbus wrote, ". . . gold is treasure, and he who possesses it does all he wishes to in this world."

In this woodcut illustration, Columbus shows a map to King Ferdinand and Queen Isabella of Spain.

TEXT: Olson, Julius E., and Edward Gaylord Bourne, eds. The Northmen, Columbus, and Cabot, 985-1503. New York: Charles Scribner's Sons, 1906.; PHOTO: (bkgd)Kompaniets Taras/Shutterstock.com, (l)Sigur/Shutterstock.com, (r)North Wind Picture Archives/Alamy Stock Photo

This illustration shows the Aztecs greeting the Spanish explorer Hernán Cortés.

Faith!

After capturing native people and taking over their land, the Spanish explorers threatened them with slavery or death if they did not swear their **allegiance** to the Catholic Church. This was called the Requirement (or *Requerimiento* in Spanish) of 1513. Of course, the native people did not speak or understand Spanish, so they did not know what they were agreeing to! But even when they did obey, they were still enslaved and mistreated by the Spanish explorers.

WordBlast

Allegiance means "loyalty." What are some ways that people show allegiance to their country?

PRIMARY SOURCE

In Their Words...

I certify to you that, with the help of God, we shall powerfully enter into your country and shall make war against you in all ways and manners that we can . . . We shall take you and your wives and your children, and shall make slaves of them, and as such shall sell and dispose of them as Their Highnesses may command. And we shall take your goods, and shall do you all the mischief and damage that we can . . . .

—*from* the Requirement of 1513, issued in the name of King Ferdinand and his daughter, Queen Juana

TEXT: Doctor Palacios Rubios. 1513. "The Requisition." In The Spanish Conquest in America, by Arthur Helps, 382. London: John W. Parker and Son, 1855.; PHOTO: (bkgd)Kompaniets Taras/Shutterstock.com, (inset)North Wind Picture Archives/Alamy Stock Photo

Navigating the Oceans

By the Stars

During the Age of Exploration, different tools were used for navigation. The stars were—and still are!—an important navigational tool. Orion, the hunter, is a very visible constellation. This star pattern helped explorers figure out their positions as they navigated the oceans.

The constellation Orion is outlined here. Do you see the figure of a hunter holding a shield and a club?

Introducing... the Astrolabe!

Would you like to use an astrolabe? This hand-held device has a moveable arm to measure the angle of a bright star above the horizon—the star's **altitude**. Rotate a metal map of stars, and you can determine time and direction, locate stars in the sky, and make other calculations!

The astrolabe shown here indicates the positions of some different bright stars. You can also predict when the Sun or certain bright stars will rise or set on any date.

WordBlast

What do you think **altitude** means? How does the text help you figure that out?

A Compass Points the Way

The compass came to Europe from China in the 1100s. The compass included a lodestone, a type of iron ore with magnetic properties. The lodestone was used to magnetize a needle, and the needle would point toward Earth's magnetic north pole. The compass became an important tool for guiding European ships across the ocean.

Unfortunately, compasses were not always reliable in the 1400s and 1500s. Ships contained many objects made of iron. Sometimes the iron caused the magnetized needles to give false readings.

LIFE AT SEA
FOR MANY SAILORS, THE WORK DAY STARTS BEFORE DAWN, BUT THE SHIP IS MANNED EVERY HOUR, DAY OR NIGHT.
EW!
THE WORST PART IS TRIPPING OVER *RATS* IN THE DARK.
AFTER SUNRISE, THE *LOOKOUT* SCANS THE HORIZON FOR SIGNS OF LAND.
A SAIL RIPPED IN THE WIND, BUT NOTHING AT SEA IS THROWN OUT IF IT CAN BE REPAIRED.
THIS SAIL WON'T BE PRETTY, BUT IT WILL GET US BACK TO OUR TOP SPEED OF *100 MILES A DAY.*
FRESH FOOD DOESN'T LAST LONG, SO SAILORS EAT A LOT OF SALTED MEAT AND FISH – HARDLY ANY FRUITS AND VEGETABLES. EVEN THE CAPTAIN CAN'T BE FUSSY.
WHY ARE YOU TAPPING THAT BISCUIT ON THE TABLE, CAPTAIN?
I WANT TO MAKE SURE ALL THE *BUGS* RUN OUT BEFORE I EAT IT.
SAILORS HAVE NO FORKS OR SPOONS. THEY USE THEIR KNIVES TO EAT. THEY DRINK WINE WITH THEIR MEAL BECAUSE FRESH WATER ON BOARD USUALLY TURNS FOUL AND SMELLY.
I LOVE ANYTHING WITH DARK MOLASSES BECAUSE IT HIDES ALL THE *MOLD!*

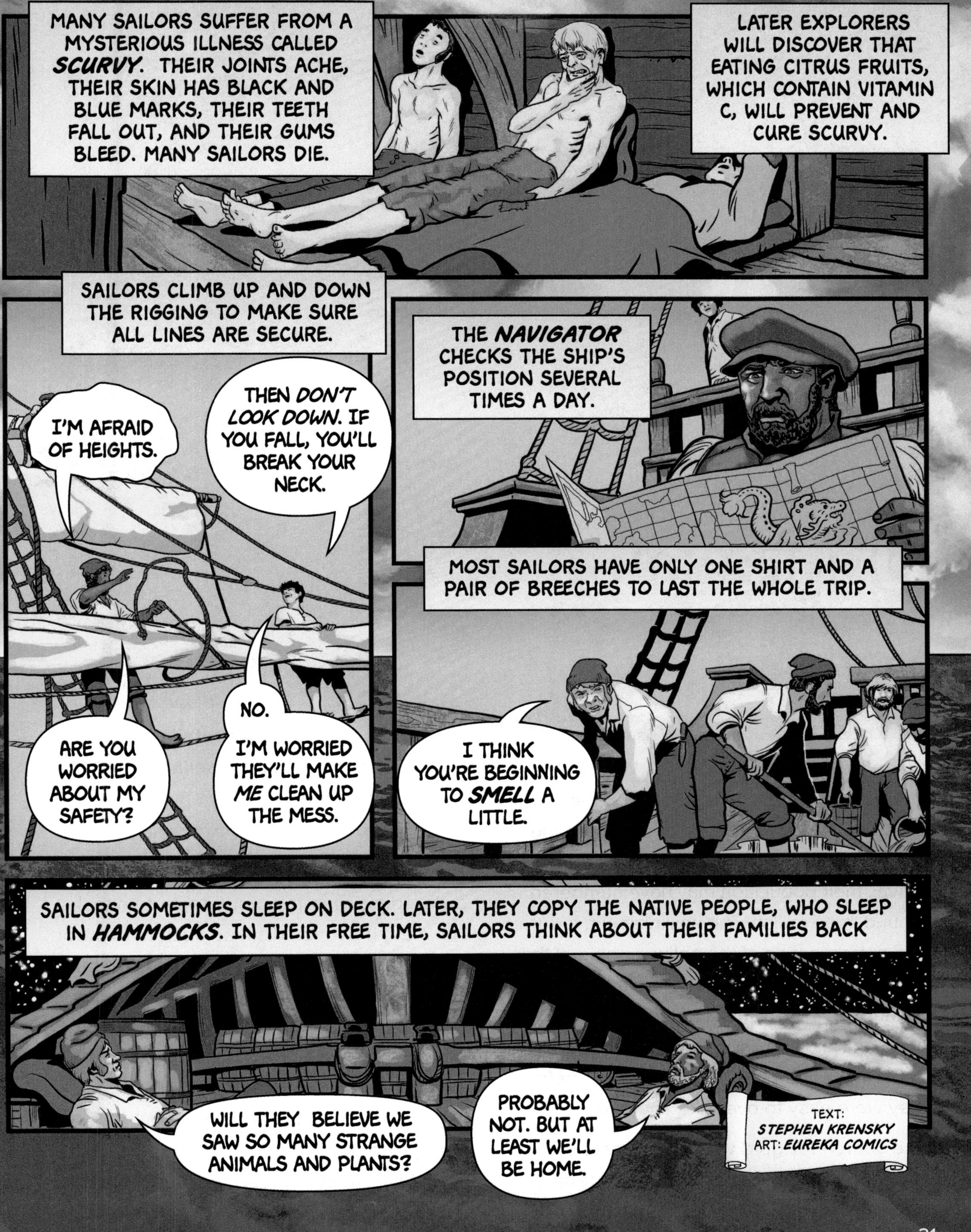
MANY SAILORS SUFFER FROM A MYSTERIOUS ILLNESS CALLED SCURVY. THEIR JOINTS ACHE, THEIR SKIN HAS BLACK AND BLUE MARKS, THEIR TEETH FALL OUT, AND THEIR GUMS BLEED. MANY SAILORS DIE.
LATER EXPLORERS WILL DISCOVER THAT EATING CITRUS FRUITS, WHICH CONTAIN VITAMIN C, WILL PREVENT AND CURE SCURVY.
SAILORS CLIMB UP AND DOWN THE RIGGING TO MAKE SURE ALL LINES ARE SECURE.
I'M AFRAID OF HEIGHTS.
THEN DON'T LOOK DOWN. IF YOU FALL, YOU'LL BREAK YOUR NECK.
ARE YOU WORRIED ABOUT MY SAFETY?
NO.
I'M WORRIED THEY'LL MAKE ME CLEAN UP THE MESS.
THE NAVIGATOR CHECKS THE SHIP'S POSITION SEVERAL TIMES A DAY.
MOST SAILORS HAVE ONLY ONE SHIRT AND A PAIR OF BREECHES TO LAST THE WHOLE TRIP.
I THINK YOU'RE BEGINNING TO SMELL A LITTLE.
SAILORS SOMETIMES SLEEP ON DECK. LATER, THEY COPY THE NATIVE PEOPLE, WHO SLEEP IN HAMMOCKS. IN THEIR FREE TIME, SAILORS THINK ABOUT THEIR FAMILIES BACK
WILL THEY BELIEVE WE SAW SO MANY STRANGE ANIMALS AND PLANTS?
PROBABLY NOT. BUT AT LEAST WE'LL BE HOME.
TEXT: STEPHEN KRENSKY
ART: EUREKA COMICS

The Oppression of the Taíno

WordBlast

What does the word **retaliation** mean? How are the words **retaliation** and **retaliate** related?

When Columbus arrived in the West Indies in 1492, he met the Taíno people for the first time. The Taíno lived in communities around the Caribbean. At the time of Columbus's arrival, their population may have numbered around three million. The enslavement, torture, and extermination of the native people of the West Indies followed quickly on the heels of Columbus and his men. Columbus noted in his journal that the Taínos were not as used to battle and warfare as the Spaniards. Therefore, they were easy to overtake and rule.

The search for gold was the primary cause for the mistreatment of the native people. On one of Columbus's later voyages, he ordered his men to complete certain tasks. His men, however, disliked such hard labor and refused to act. When Columbus returned, he punished the natives for the failure of his own men. He blamed them for destroying the settlers' property, stealing their food, and instilling fear. In **retaliation** for these acts, few—if any—of which had actually occurred, he had his men round up over 1,500 Taíno men, women, and children, and forced them into slavery.

Atelier Sommerland/Shutterstock.com

Columbus, in need of a cargo other than gold and spices to ship to Spain, decided to send the Taíno slaves as a show of the wealth available in the New World. He loaded the "best men and women" onto ships and sent them off to Europe, thus beginning the widespread enslavement of the native peoples.

As more Spanish colonies were established in the Caribbean, the Taíno were forced to work in gold mines and on plantations. Many starved when they were not allowed to plant their own crops. Others died because they had no resistance to diseases carried by the Europeans. By the mid-1500s, the Taíno communities had been reduced to only a few survivors.

CONNECT THROUGH LITERATURE

from The Encounter

by **Jane Yolen**

In 1492, a young Taíno boy dreams of three great-winged birds with sharp teeth that ride the ocean waves near his home. When he wakes up, the birds are floating in the sea—three ships full of strange men. While the boy believes his dream is a sign of danger, the chief of his people welcomes the strangers.

So we built a great feasting fire and readied the pepper pot and yams and cassava bread and fresh fish. For though the strangers were not quite human beings, we would still treat them as such.

Our chief rolled tobacco leaves and showed them how to smoke, but they coughed and snorted and clearly did not know about these simple things.

Then I leaned forward and stared into their chief's eyes. They were blue and gray like the shifting sea.

Suddenly, I remembered my dream and stared at each of the strangers in turn. Even those with dark human eyes looked away, like dogs before they are driven from the fire.

So I drew back from the feast, which is not what one should do, and I watched how the sky strangers touched our golden nose rings and our golden armbands but not the flesh of our faces or arms. I watched their chief smile. It was the serpent's smile—no lips and all teeth.

I jumped up, crying, "Do not welcome them." But the welcome had already been given.

THEN AND NOW

Mapping a Voyage

From 1577 to 1580, the English seaman Francis Drake sailed around the world. He became the first English explorer to **circumnavigate** the globe. At the secret request of Queen Elizabeth I, he captured treasure from Spanish ships and Spanish settlements along the way. He also claimed California for the Queen, naming it Nova Albion. Upon his return to England in 1580, Drake was knighted by Queen Elizabeth and hailed as a hero. The Spanish, on the other hand, called him a pirate!

The maps that Drake used did not have detailed information about all the places he visited. When Drake returned to England, he gave the Queen his journal, which included his own charts, sketches, and maps from the voyage. This journal, which later disappeared, was used to create updated maps of the world like the one below.

WordBlast

In Latin, *circum* means "around". Use this clue to figure out the meaning of **circumnavigate**. Check your answer with a dictionary.

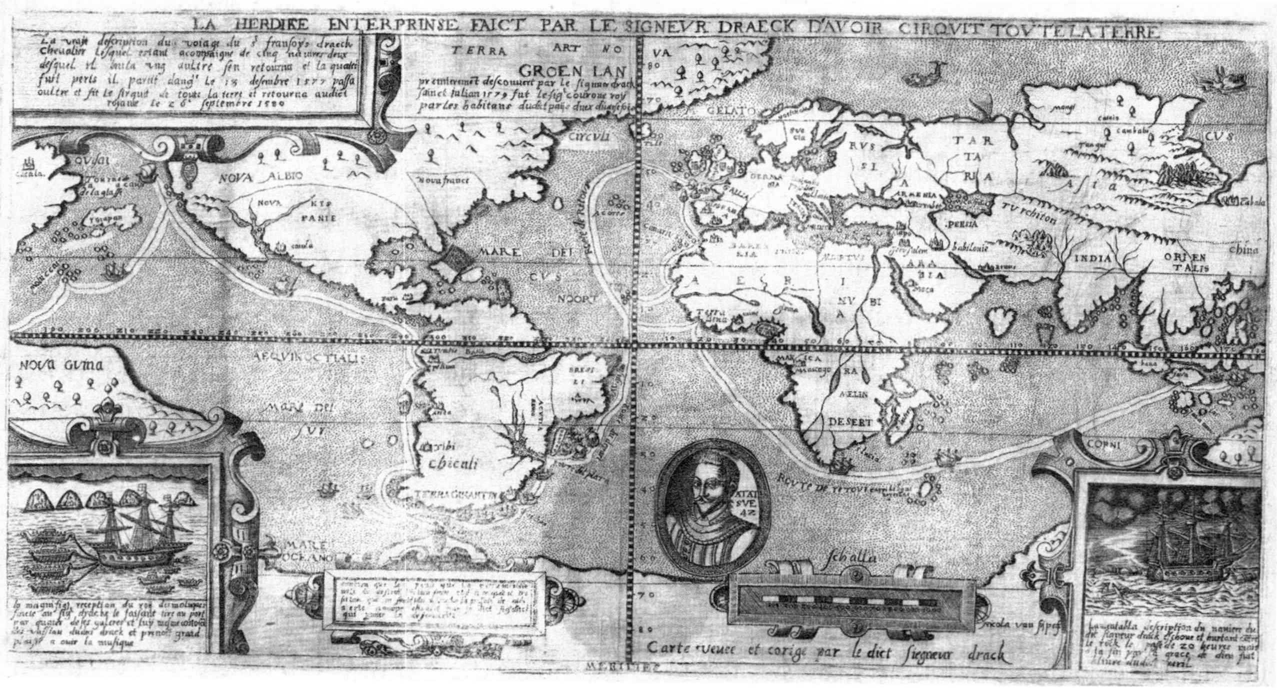

This map of Drake's voyage was created around 1581 by a Dutch mapmaker, Nicola van Sype.

EXPLORE the Maps!

With a partner, look closely at the older map.

- What details do you notice?
- How does the mapmaker show the route of Drake's voyage?
- Trace the route with your finger. What places can you identify?

Compare the older map with the modern world map.

- In what ways are the two maps the same?
- What might be some reasons for the differences on the two maps?

What are some questions you have about the older map? With your partner, figure out how you could find answers to these questions.

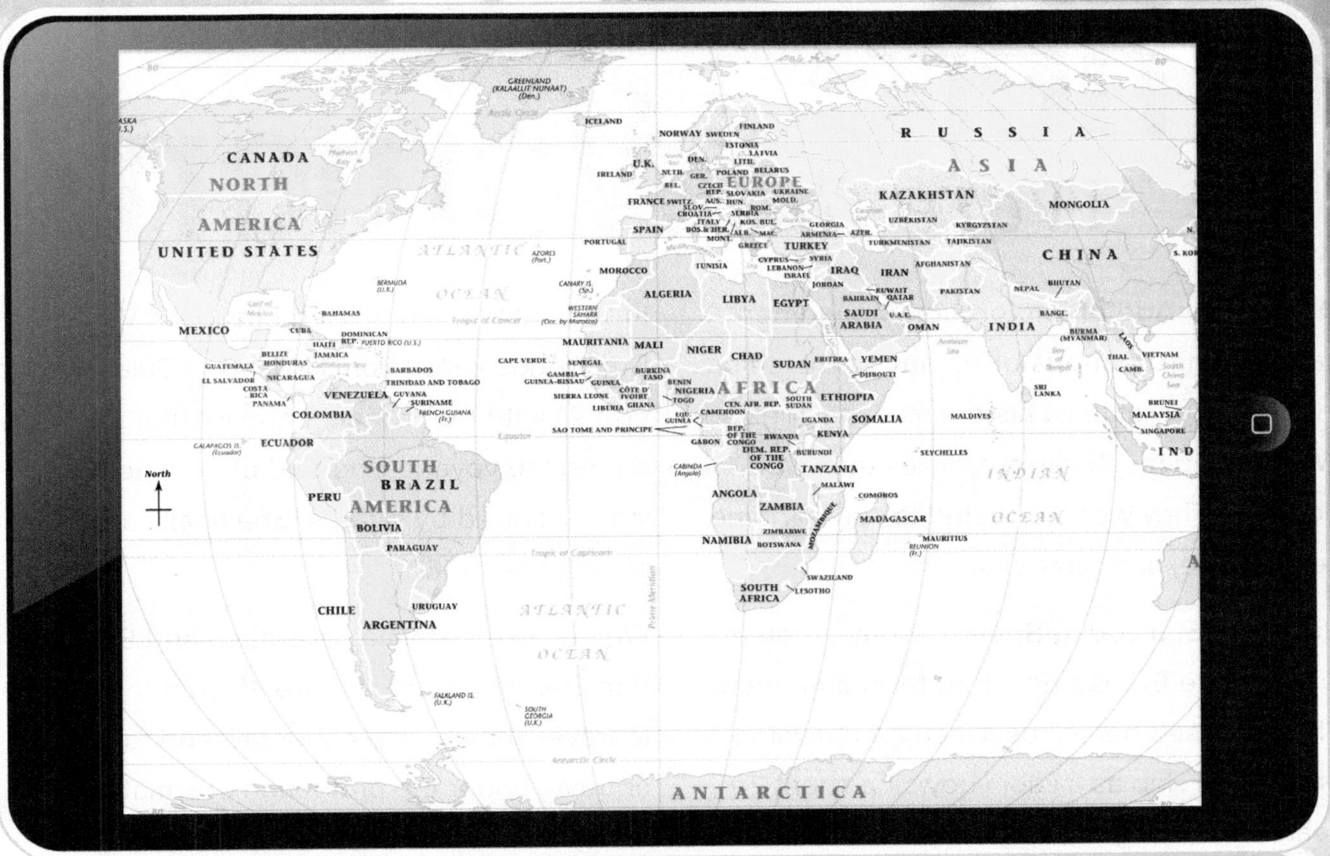

(bkgd)Pakhnyushchy/Shutterstock.com, (t)Stephen Rees/Shutterstock.com, (b)McGraw-Hill Education, (inset)Antenna Audio, Inc./Getty Images

Christopher Columbus is received by King Ferdinand and Queen Isabella upon his arrival in Spain in 1500.

Where *Were the* Women?

During the Age of Exploration, no women sailed with Columbus or on any of the ships in the 1500s—at least historians don't think so. Women had much narrower lives than women do today. They were expected to stay at home, keep house, and raise children.

But in 1605, a young Spanish woman named Catalina de Erauso escaped from a convent. She disguised herself as a man and traveled on board a ship as a cabin boy. She spent 20 years wandering around the world.

In 1676, a woman named Elizabeth Van Der Woude sailed from Holland to Guiana at age 21 with her father. In the journal she kept during the voyage, she told of how her ship was captured by pirates. She finally arrived back home in 1677.

Women like Catalina de Erauso and Elizabeth Van Der Woude were rare. If women wanted to travel, they had to either pretend to be men or travel under the protection of a male family member. Most women remained at home.

This engraving shows Queen Elizabeth I knighting Sir Francis Drake after he circumnavigated the globe.

However, two extremely powerful women played significant roles during the Age of Exploration: Queen Elizabeth I of England and Queen Isabella of Spain. Neither of them ever traveled very far from home, but their money and influence supported many of the most famous explorers of the time. Queen Elizabeth knighted Sir Francis Drake when he returned from sailing around the world. Queen Isabella helped pay for the voyages of Christopher Columbus.

It would be a long time before women were free to travel and explore. But that, of course, has changed. These women were very brave for that time in history. There always will be women who take chances and make changes in the world!

Citizenship IN OUR DAY

Explorer LONNIE DUPRE

Lonnie Dupre is a real-world explorer! He has traveled in some of the coldest places in the world. And he has found that climate change is hurting the Earth, our home.

Lonnie Dupre launched One World Endeavors, which has one goal: to spread the word about how important the Arctic region is for the well-being of the whole planet. Its primary efforts are to inspire worldwide movements dedicated both to fighting pollution and to addressing climate change.

"For as long as I can remember, I have loved snow and ice. As a result, I have spent most of my life exploring the Arctic region. These journeys have brought such joy and beauty to my life that I have dedicated myself to helping preserve these wonderful frozen places. More than ever before, I am driven to share my passion for the Arctic, a region whose health and stability have far-reaching consequences for us all . . . ."

— Lonnie Dupre

EXPLORATION DOESN'T HAVE TO STOP!
YOU CAN BE AN EXPLORER, TOO! JUST ASK LONNIE DUPRE!

TEXT: Lonnie Dupre/One World Endeavors. PHOTO: (t)Lonnie Dupre/One World Endeavors, (b)Volodymyr Goinyk/Shutterstock.com

Take Action!

More to Explore

What else are you curious about? Here are more questions that you can research and discuss.

Who are some other early explorers you would like to learn more about?

How did the native peoples of the Americas view the European explorers?

What present-day explorers do you find interesting? What are they exploring?

WordBlast

- How did Sir Francis Drake show his **allegiance** to Queen Elizabeth I?
- Do you think the **altitude** of a star can change? Explain your reasoning.
- What are some ways that people **circumnavigate** the globe today?
- Do you think Columbus's **retaliation** against the Taíno was fair? Why or why not?

ESSENTIAL QUESTION EQ

Reflect

What happened when diverse cultures crossed paths?

Chapter 3

A Changing Continent

ESSENTIAL QUESTION EQ

How did European settlements impact North America?

Table of Contents

A Colonial House

This kitchen in a Philadelphia house dating from around 1740 has features typical of a colonial home.

- What materials were used in this colonial kitchen?
- What types of utensils were used?
- What do the details in the kitchen tell you about life in colonial America?

Hard Times in Jamestown

TEXT: *STEPHEN KRENSKY*
ART: *EUREKA COMICS*

104 ENGLISH MEN AND BOYS ARRIVE IN VIRGINIA IN 1607. THEY FIND A PLACE FOR A SETTLEMENT AND NAME IT *JAMESTOWN*, AFTER THEIR KING.
I HOPE WE ARE SAFER ON LAND THAN WE WERE AT SEA!
OUR NEW FORT SHOULD PROTECT US.
THE SETTLEMENT NEEDS FARMERS AND TRADESPEOPLE TO SUCCEED. BUT MOST OF THE COLONISTS ARE NOT USED TO HARD WORK.
I'M GOING TO FIND GOLD RIGHT AWAY AND TAKE IT BACK TO ENGLAND.
ME TOO!
FORTUNATELY, THEY ARE ABLE TO TRADE SOME EUROPEAN GOODS FOR CORN WITH THE NEARBY *POWHATAN INDIANS*.
WE COULD GROW BETTER CROPS IF WE WEREN'T IN A DROUGHT.
NOTHING IS EASY. MANY SETTLERS DIE OF DISEASE. IN JANUARY, 1608, A FIRE DESTROYS CORN FROM THE POWHATAN INDIANS AND FRESH SUPPLIES FROM ENGLAND.
JUST WHEN WE HAD ENOUGH FOOD . . .
THE SETTLERS REBUILD JAMESTOWN, BUT THERE STILL ISN'T ENOUGH FOOD. THEN 300 NEW COLONISTS ARRIVE IN AUGUST, 1609. THEY HAVE SURVIVED A HURRICANE, BUT THEIR SUPPLIES WERE LOST.
WE DON'T HAVE MUCH, BUT WE'LL SHARE WHAT WE HAVE.
WE ARE LUCKY TO BE ALIVE.
AT LEAST FOR NOW.

THE DROUGHT HAS AFFECTED FOOD SUPPLIES. THE INDIANS FEEL THREATENED BY THE COLONISTS' DEMANDS FOR MORE CORN. CHIEF POWHATAN ORDERS AN ATTACK ON ANY COLONISTS FOUND OUTSIDE THE FORT.
I WISH WE COULD GO OUT AND LOOK FOR FOOD.
THE WINTER OF 1609-1610 WILL LATER BE KNOWN AS THE *STARVING TIME*.
WE BARELY HAVE ENOUGH FOOD FOR ONE MEAL A DAY.
SUPPLIES WILL STILL RUN OUT BY MIDWINTER.
SOME SETTLERS BEGIN EATING THEIR SHOES. DOGS AND CATS DISAPPEAR.
WHAT ARE YOU EATING?
I DON'T WANT TO TALK ABOUT IT.
ONLY 60 COLONISTS SURVIVE UNTIL SPRING. WHEN A SHIP ARRIVES IN MAY, THE COLONISTS DECIDE TO ABANDON JAMESTOWN. BUT AS THEY SAIL AWAY, THEY MEET THE SHIP OF THEIR NEW GOVERNOR. PLANS CHANGE.
WE WERE ON OUR WAY HOME TO ENGLAND!
THE NEW GOVERNOR HAS ORDERED US TO RETURN TO JAMESTOWN.
OVER THE NEXT FEW YEARS, MORE PEOPLE ARRIVE. NEW GOVERNORS BRING HARSH LAWS TO JAMESTOWN. THERE ARE FREQUENT WARS WITH THE INDIANS. LIFE IS DIFFICULT, BUT THE COLONY GROWS.
I STILL HAVEN'T MADE MY FORTUNE.
ME NEITHER. BUT AT LEAST I'M GETTING ENOUGH TO EAT.

The Great Pumpkin

by **Phyllis Mussman**

The Great Pumpkin—best supporting actor in the Thanksgiving feast of New England Pilgrims, right? Everyone knows that. But not everyone knows that pumpkins, or “pompions,” as they were called, along with corn and beans, helped keep Jamestown settlers alive.

In the seventeenth century, English people did not say, “Pumpkins! Yum!” They said, “Pompions! Yuck!” Pumpkinlike vegetables were thought to be fit only for cattle, hogs, and the poorest people. That included many of the first Jamestown settlers. They were kept alive during the first two winters by fish and game, corn bread, Virginia peas, and pumpkins grown by Native Americans who lived nearby.

Settlers soon learned that American Indian farmers grew pumpkins for medicines, too. Some believed that a mixture of pumpkin seeds and watermelon seeds would heal wounds. Ground pumpkin stems brewed into a tea were said to cure other ailments. Today we know that a mere one-half cup of canned pumpkin has more than five times the suggested daily allowance of Vitamin A, with a fair amount of potassium and iron, in just forty-one calories.

The colonists finally caught on, and soon pumpkin was everywhere. It was dried, stewed, baked, and roasted. As the "starving time" and other hardships eventually gave way to times of peace and plenty, so did the lowly pompion rise from the barnyard to become The Great Pumpkin.

Pumpkins were not only food, but the American Indians grew them for medicines too.

The Swedish
Log Cabin

Log cabins—simple, cozy, yet primitive shelters—seem like the most American of homes. Abraham Lincoln grew up in one. Countless pioneers built log cabins on the frontier in the 1800s. Interestingly, the American log cabin may have been brought over by the Swedes. Swedish colonists established their first colony in America in 1638, settling near the Delaware River.

Back home in Sweden, log cabins were a practical home style since Scandinavia's forests were full of softwoods (conifers such as pine and spruce). Bringing building materials from Europe on small sailing ships would have been impossible. But America's forests offered a plentiful supply of logs for cabins.

The classic Swedish log cabin was built of split logs complete with bark. The logs were notched at each end so they fit together, making nails unnecessary. Gaps between the logs were filled with chinking: mud or clay mixed with straw, grass, or animal hair. Sliding boards covered windows. The cabin had a stone corner fireplace and clay floors. It usually had one room and one or one-and-a-half stories.

In the 1800s, thousands of Americans settled in the West. Once again, log cabins were a practical housing solution. Shipping building supplies by horseback or wagon was not **feasible**. So pioneers built log cabins with the resources at hand. One man could construct a cabin in one to two weeks! Log cabins became a symbol of American simplicity and democracy. Most important, Americans, like the Swedes, found that the log cabin was a practical choice for a solid, easily constructed home.

ladyenvy09/iStock/Getty Images

WordBlast

What is the meaning of **feasible**? How does the text help you figure that out?

William Dean Howells

CONNECT THROUGH LITERATURE

from My Year in a Log Cabin

William Dean Howells, 1893

William Dean Howells was a famous American novelist and playwright. When he was twelve, his family moved into a log cabin for a year. Later in life he wrote a memoir about that experience.

Our cabin stood close upon the road, but behind it broadened a cornfield of eighty acres. They still built log-cabins for dwellings in that region forty years ago, but ours must have been nearly half a century old when we went into it. . . .

The cabin, rude as it was, was not without its sophistications, its concessions to the spirit of modern luxury. The logs it was built of had not been left rounded, as they grew, but had been squared in a saw-mill, and the crevices between them had not been chinked with moss and daubed with clay in the true pioneer fashion, but had been neatly plastered with mortar, and the chimney, instead of being a structure of clay-covered sticks, was solidly laid in courses of stone.

TEXT: Howells, William Dean. My Year in a Log Cabin. New York: Harper & Brothers, 1893.; PHOTO: (l)Chronicle/Alamy Stock Photo, (r)Todd Gipstein/National Geographic/Getty Images

Deadly Diseases

The story of colonial America includes the story of disease. Settlers and Native Americans fought wars and died of starvation. But the greatest enemy, for both sides, was disease.

New World settlers arrived in ships that were cramped, disease-ridden, and filthy. Passengers were exposed to infectious diseases such as typhus, dysentery, and the bubonic plague. Many also suffered from scurvy, caused by a lack of Vitamin C, because they had no fresh fruits or vegetables on their long journeys. Once across the Atlantic, living conditions in the colonies contributed to illness. For example, colonists in Massachusetts were not ready for the frigid winters. Settlers in Virginia were unprepared for the hot, muggy climate. Mosquitoes carried **microbes** that caused yellow fever and malaria. Thousands of settlers died from disease, usually within two years of their arrival.

WordBlast

The prefix micro- means "small." How does this help you figure out the meaning of microbes? How does the text help you verify the meaning?

PRIMARY SOURCE

In Their Words...

But that which was most sadd & lamentable was, that in 2. or 3. moneths time halfe of their company dyed, espetialy in Jan: & February, being ye depth of winter, and wanting houses & other comforts; being infected with ye scurvie & other diseases, which this long vioage & their inacomodate condition had brought upon them; so as ther dyed some times 2. or 3. of a day, in ye foresaid time; that of 100. & odd persons, scarce 50. remained.

—from *Of Plymouth Plantation* by William Bradford

TEXT: Bradford, William. Bradford's History "Of Plimoth Plantation." Boston

Disease was the major reason the Native American population decreased so dramatically in the first hundred years after the arrival of the European settlers. Before colonization, many illnesses that were common in the countries of Europe did not exist in the Americas. For centuries, this worked to the advantage of those, like the Indians, who lived in the New World. As long as they were not exposed to measles, typhus, or smallpox, Native Americans probably were healthier than Europeans.

The arrival of Europeans in the New World, however, changed that. Early settlers and explorers brought with them different and deadly diseases. Since Europeans had battled these illnesses for generations, many had built up protection against those that were relatively mild, such as influenza and the mumps.

In North America, though, these diseases encountered a population with no resistance power. American Indians had no immunity to the measles. Very few survived the plague or the mumps. Common European diseases swept through the New World, devastating Native American populations. For example, the Patuxet Indians lived around Plymouth Harbor. Even before the Pilgrims arrived in Massachusetts, as many as nine out of ten Patuxets died after being exposed to disease. In Virginia, there were around 25,000 Powhatan Indians in the Jamestown area before Europeans settled there. After European settlement, many died of diseases such as smallpox and influenza, leaving a population of only about 15,000.

New arrivals to settlements such as Plymouth Plantation brought with them deadly diseases.

In the southern colonies, enslaved African Americans often worked in the fields.

Freedom Beckons

European colonists started a new way of life when they moved to America. They worked to build successful communities, farms, and businesses. They soon found that they needed many workers to realize their ambitions. The first enslaved Africans were brought to America in 1619. Their labor was used to build the American colonies.

In the North, enslaved Africans were put to work on farms and in manufacturing firms and other companies. In the South, most enslaved people worked on farms, helping to produce crops such as tobacco.

Most Africans and their descendants in Colonial America were enslaved their entire lives. But sometimes enslaved people won their freedom. Here are the stories of three who did.

Lucy Terry Prince

Born in West Africa around 1730, Lucy Terry was kidnapped and brought to America as an infant. At age five, she was sold to a settler in the frontier town of Deerfield, Massachusetts. In 1746, she survived an Indian attack and later wrote a poem in memory of the townspeople who died. Ten years later, she married Abijah Prince, a landowner who was formerly enslaved, who purchased her freedom.

The mother of seven children, Prince acquired a reputation for **eloquence**. She used her speaking skills to fight for her children's right to a good education. She once argued a case before the Vermont Supreme Court. She died in 1821.

Yarrow Mamout

Yarrow Mamout was born in Africa in the early 1700s. As a young man, he was kidnapped and sold overseas to a Maryland slaveholder. Freed by his slaveholder widow when his slaveholder died, he worked hard and eventually bought a house and other property in Georgetown, near the nation's new capital. Mamout lived to be more than one hundred years old. He followed the teachings of the prophet Muhammad throughout his life.

Yarrow Mamout won his freedom and eventually bought a house and other property near the nation's new capital.

James Armistead spied for the Americans during the Revolution.

James Lafayette

Born in Virginia in the late 1740s, James Lafayette was given the name James Armistead, the surname of his slaveholder. In 1781, the Revolutionary War was raging. Armistead volunteered for spy duty under the Marquis de Lafayette (a French general and statesman, who served from 1771–1781 in the Continental army in the American Revolution). Working as a double agent, Armistead provided valuable reports to the patriots that helped them win the war at Yorktown.

At the end of the war, Armistead was still enslaved. In 1786, the Virginia legislature granted him his freedom, thanks in part to a testimonial from the Marquis de Lafayette. Once free, Armistead changed his name to Lafayette. He bought a farm in Virginia and received a pension for his war service. James Lafayette died in 1830.

WordBlast

What is the meaning of **eloquence?** How does the text help you figure that out?

Archeologists excavate an area of the fort at Historic Jamestown.

Excavating Colonial Sites

Suppose your job was digging up sites where the first European colonists settled in America. You might find a piece of pottery, a metal tool, animal bones, or even a solid gold ring. You may think a valuable piece of jewelry would be the most exciting discovery. To an archeologist, a bone or a spoon might be just as thrilling.

Archeologists study history by **excavating** sites. They analyze artifacts and other objects in the ground to learn more about a community. Some important archeological sites in America are those of early colonies such as Jamestown, Roanoke, and Plymouth.

Archeologists continue to investigate Plymouth colony, collecting artifacts such as stoneware, nails, and metal tools. They investigate building ruins to learn more about the Pilgrims' architecture and way of life. Archeologists continue to tell us more about early Americans, one nail or shoe at a time.

Archeological tools such as these are used in excavation colonial sites.

WordBlast

What is the meaning of **excavating?** How do the text and the word's prefix help you figure that out?

Take Action!

More to Explore

Find out more about ways in which European colonization affected North America. Here are some questions to guide you.

When European settlers came to North America, what other foods did the American Indians introduce to them?

What were some home styles of colonists in the New World? How did settlers from different countries influence these styles?

How have the diseases contracted by European settlers and American Indians become less deadly with time?

WordBlast

- Why might **eloquence** be an important factor in a person's success?
- What types of objects do archeologists find when **excavating** sites?
- Why was a log cabin more **feasible** than other types of dwellings in the colonies?
- What aspects of colonial settlers' lives made contracting dangerous **microbes** more likely?

ESSENTIAL EQ QUESTION

Reflect

How did European settlements impact North America?

Chapter 4
The Road to WAR

ESSENTIAL QUESTION (EQ)

Why would a nation want to become independent?

Table of Contents

A Cartoon Commentary

"The Repeal, Or the Funeral of Miss Americ-Stamp" by Benjamin Wilson (March 18, 1766)

While this famous political cartoon may look like a sad scene, it is actually celebrating a victory for England's North American colonists. In the cartoon, British leaders attend a "funeral" in London for the Stamp Act—a British tax on all paper documents in the colonies. The tax was repealed by Parliament in 1766.

Look closely at the political cartoon.

- Why would these British leaders be sad about the repeal of the Stamp Act?
- Why would North American colonists enjoy this cartoon?

Game of War

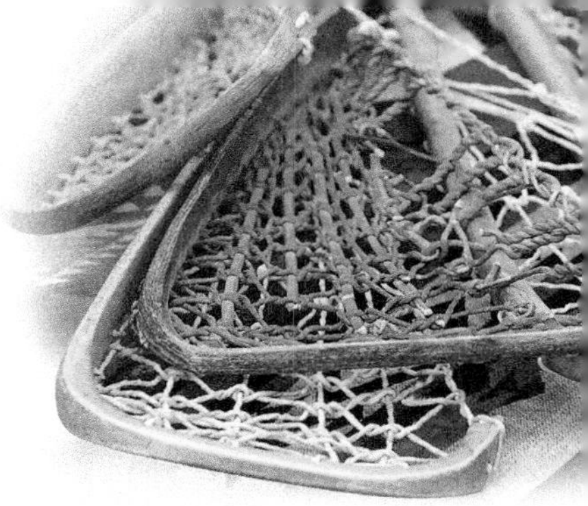

Did you know that in the past, American Indians sometimes settled arguments by playing a game of lacrosse? When Europeans arrived in the Americas, they were fascinated by the game. However, as the British would discover in 1763, lacrosse was more than just a game to some American Indian tribes. It was *war*.

Styles of Play

Different American Indian tribes preferred to play lacrosse using different rules and styles of play. The number of players and the length of the field depended on the tribe or tribes involved. One detail, though, always stayed the same: the game was intense. It blurred the lines between the lacrosse field and the battlefield. Some American Indians believed that lacrosse's **ferocity** resembled a type of battle training.

A Game with Stakes

One of the most famous lacrosse games in history proved that the sport did indeed end disputes. But this time, things did not end quite peacefully. In 1763, British soldiers were stationed at Fort Michilimackinac on the eastern shore of Lake Michigan. Local American Indian tribes wanted the British invaders off their land, so they came up with a plan.

The tribesmen set up a lacrosse game—right by the walls of the fort. The British soldiers, curious, left their posts to watch the game. But the players had brought more than their lacrosse equipment. The warriors stormed the fort, weapons drawn. Britain lost Fort Michilimackinac that day.

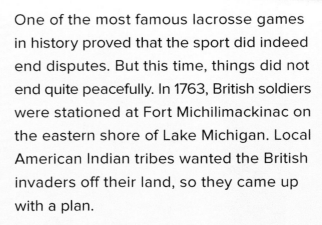

WordBlast

What is the meaning of **ferocity**? What clues from the text help you know the meaning of the word?

EXPLORE the Map

With a partner, look closely at the map.

- Which details from the text can you find on the map?
- Why was the fort's location useful for the British?
- Look at the map. Where was Fort Detroit in relation to Fort Michilimackinac?

What are some questions you have about the map? With your partner, figure out how you could find answers to these questions.

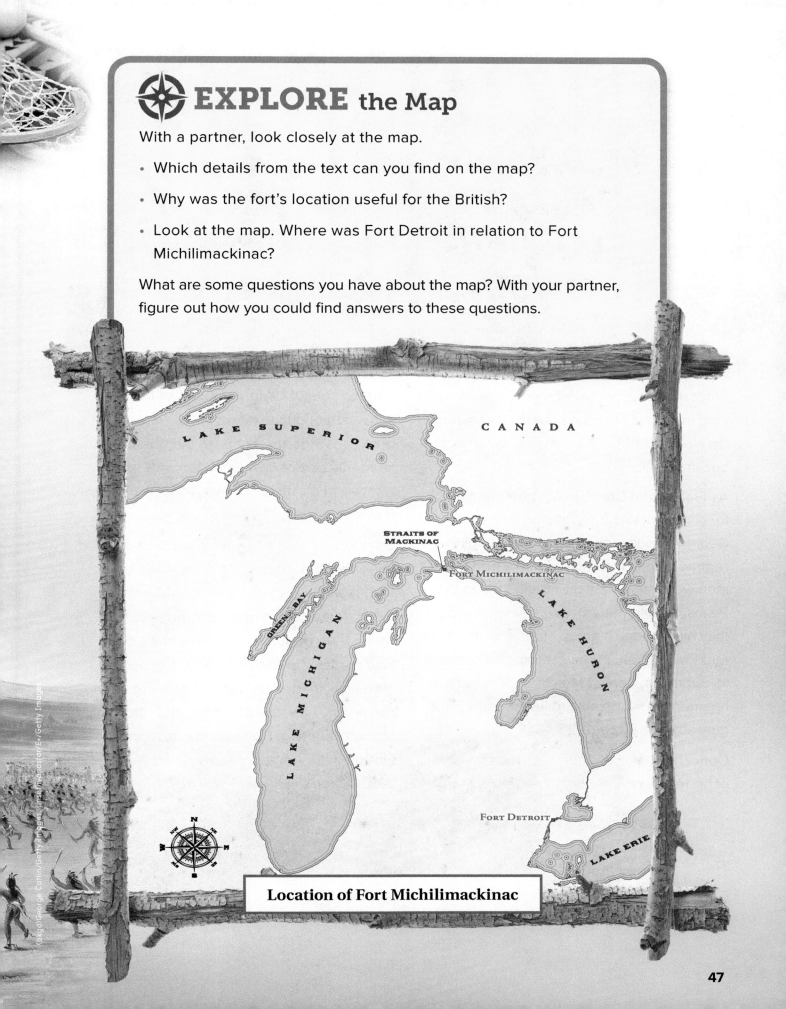

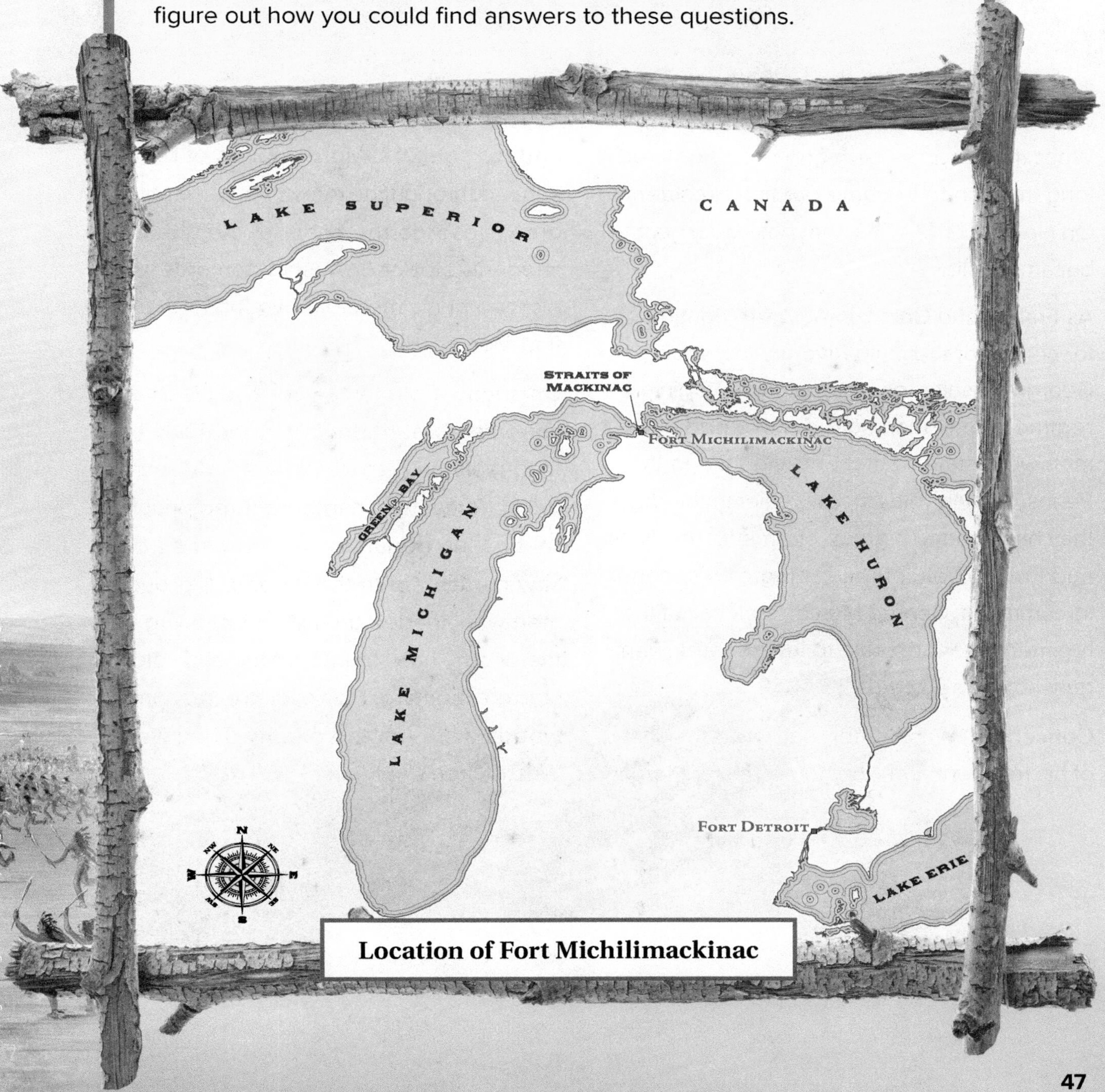

Location of Fort Michilimackinac

Danger in the Forest

What if George Washington had not lived long enough to become our first president? On November 12, 1758, that possibility nearly became reality.

As France and Great Britain were fighting for control of the Ohio River Valley, young George Washington was leading a Virginia regiment of British soldiers. He and his men were stationed at Fort Ligonier in the Pennsylvanian wilderness. Earlier in the day, they had spotted a group of American Indians and French soldiers. Washington's second-in-command, George Mercer, took half of the regiment into the forest to investigate. Then gunshots were heard.

Concerned, Washington gathered the rest of his regiment and went to search for Mercer and his soldiers. More sounds of battle echoed through the forest. As Washington drew closer to the fighting, the gunfire suddenly stopped. Washington ordered a group of his men to move forward and find Mercer.

Up ahead, Colonel Mercer and his troops were celebrating their victory. They had fought off the French soldiers and American Indian forces and captured three prisoners. As the sun began to set, Mercer's troops saw movement in the woods. A group of men was headed their way. Believing that the enemy had returned, Mercer's soldiers started shooting. However, the men in the woods were not the enemy. They were Washington's soldiers!

Washington's men were being fired on. They saw the prisoners in Mercer's camp and thought they had come across a troop of French and American Indians. So they fired back. When Washington arrived, he noticed something odd. The "enemies" on the other side were speaking English. He took a closer look and recognized a soldier from his regiment.

Washington ordered his troops to stop shooting, but many could not hear him over the loud gunfire. With the lives of all his soldiers at risk, Washington rushed into the crossfire. He stopped his men from shooting each other, and he walked away unharmed. Years later, Washington reflected on that day, claiming that his life "was in as much **jeopardy** as it has ever been before or since."

WordBlast

Jeopardy means "in danger." The suffix *-ize* means "to cause to be." What do you think the word *jeopardize* means? Verify your answer using a dictionary.

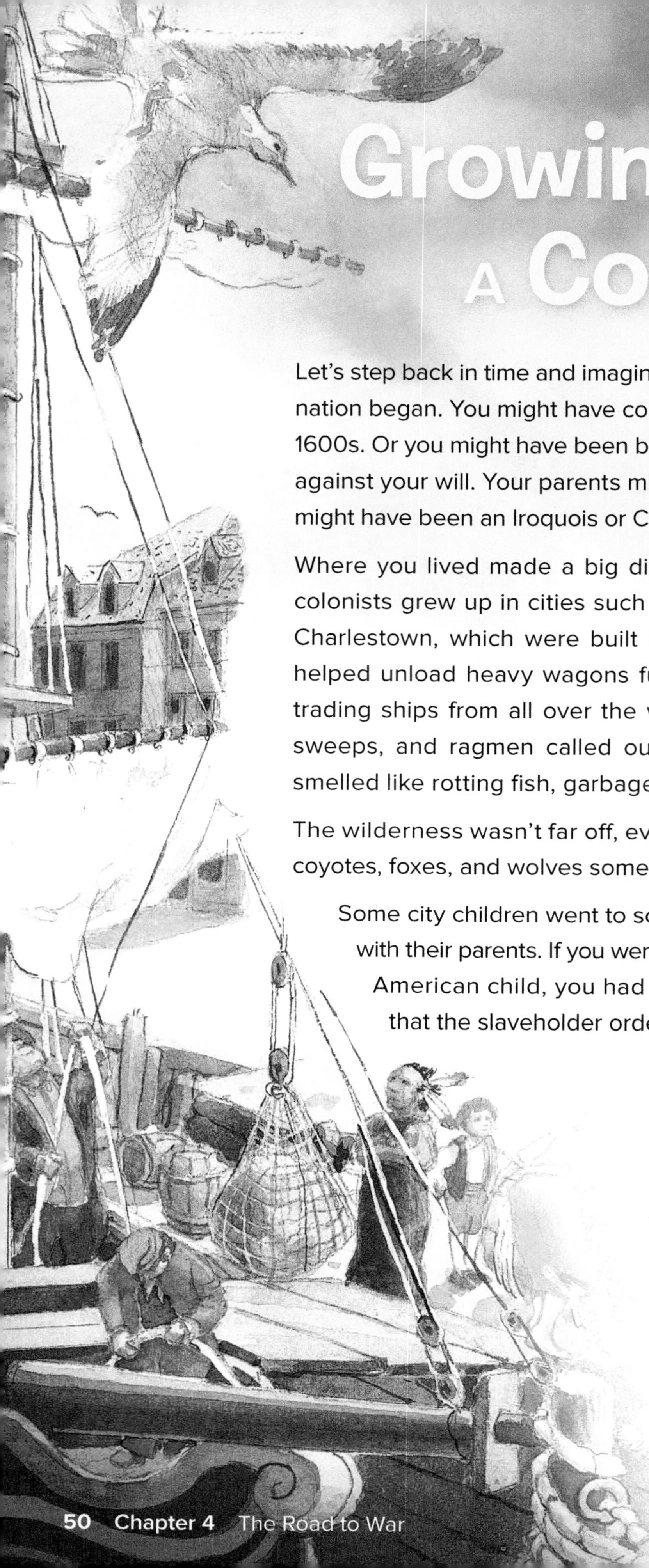

Growing Up in a Colonial City

Let's step back in time and imagine our lives as American children when our nation began. You might have come from an English family, here since the 1600s. Or you might have been born in Africa, brought here on a slave ship against your will. Your parents might have been Dutch or German. Or you might have been an Iroquois or Cherokee, one of the very first Americans.

Where you lived made a big difference in how you lived. Many young colonists grew up in cities such as Boston, New York, Philadelphia, and Charlestown, which were built near deep harbors. There, young boys helped unload heavy wagons full of lumber, tobacco, and rice into tall trading ships from all over the world. Peddlers, barrelmakers, chimney sweeps, and ragmen called out in the streets. In most cities, the air smelled like rotting fish, garbage, and the leftovers of everyday life.

The wilderness wasn't far off, even in cities such as Philadelphia. Bears, coyotes, foxes, and wolves sometimes roamed the streets.

Some city children went to school, but many worked with their parents. If you were an enslaved African American child, you had to do any work that the slaveholder ordered you to do.

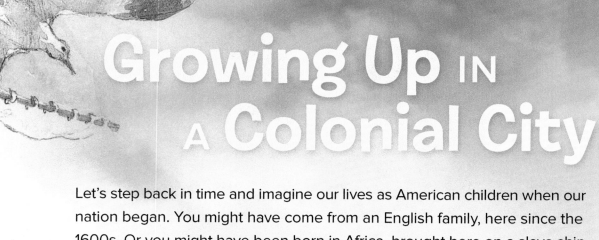

(bkgd spread)kzww/Shutterstock.com, (b)David Stuckel/Alamy Stock Photo

Young colonists were involved in the struggle for independence in many different ways. A number of teenagers participated in the Boston Tea Party in 1773.

In the evening, women and children sat on the front steps of their houses or walked to a small open area (called a "common," because it was shared land). There, children rolled large wooden hoops or played ninepin (like bowling), marbles, hopscotch, and leapfrog. The men gathered at local taverns to argue about war and independence.

Young people were aware of the conflicts between the American colonists and the British. They may have dreamed of independence and freedom. But could they imagine the **generations** of Americans who would follow them?

WordBlast

A **generation** is all of the people who are born and live around the same time period. Compare your generation with the generation of children growing up during the American Revolution. What are some similarities and differences?

All in the Family

As tensions grew between Great Britain and its North American colonies, so too did tensions grow within many colonial families. Even the members of one of the most famous families in American history found themselves at odds with each other. John Adams and Samuel Adams were second cousins, members of a prominent family in Massachusetts. While they both supported the cause of independence, they disagreed on how to reach that goal. Abigail Adams, John's wife, also had strong opinions about the future of the American colonies.

Samuel Adams (1722–1803)

As one of the first **revolutionaries**, Samuel Adams spent most of his life fighting for freedom from British control. He believed in taking action and he participated in many protests, including those against the Stamp Act. He was quick to blame the British soldiers for the Boston Massacre in 1770. Following the Massacre, Samuel rallied more people to action. He later signed the Declaration of Independence and became governor of Massachusetts.

Samuel Adams fought for freedom from British control.

WordBlast

What is the meaning of **revolutionaries?** How does the text help you figure out its meaning?

John Adams (1735–1826)

John Adams believed in peaceful law and order.

Like his second cousin Samuel Adams, John Adams also supported the colonies in their struggle against the British. However, John Adams believed in peaceful law and order instead of the vocal protests made by his cousin. As a lawyer, John did not approve of Samuel's "mob" tactics. He did not blame the British soldiers for the Boston Massacre, but instead believed the crowd was at fault for inciting the bloodshed. Nonetheless, John Adams stayed true to the colonists in their fight for independence. John went on to become the second president of the United States.

Abigail Adams (1744–1818)

"The Sword is now our only, yet dreadful alternative," wrote Abigail Adams in 1775. She, like her husband John Adams, did not wish for conflict. However, as it became increasingly clear that war was coming, Abigail remained a Patriot. She had hope in a new government—one in which women had a voice. As an opponent of slavery, Abigail also saw an opportunity to free "those who have as good a right to freedom as we have."

Abigail Adams had hope in a new government.

TEXT: (t)"Abigail Adams to Mercy Otis Warren, 3 February 1775," Founders Online, National Archives, (b)"Abigail Adams to John Adams, 22 September 1774," Founders Online, National Archives; PHOTOS: Courtesy National Gallery of Art, Washington

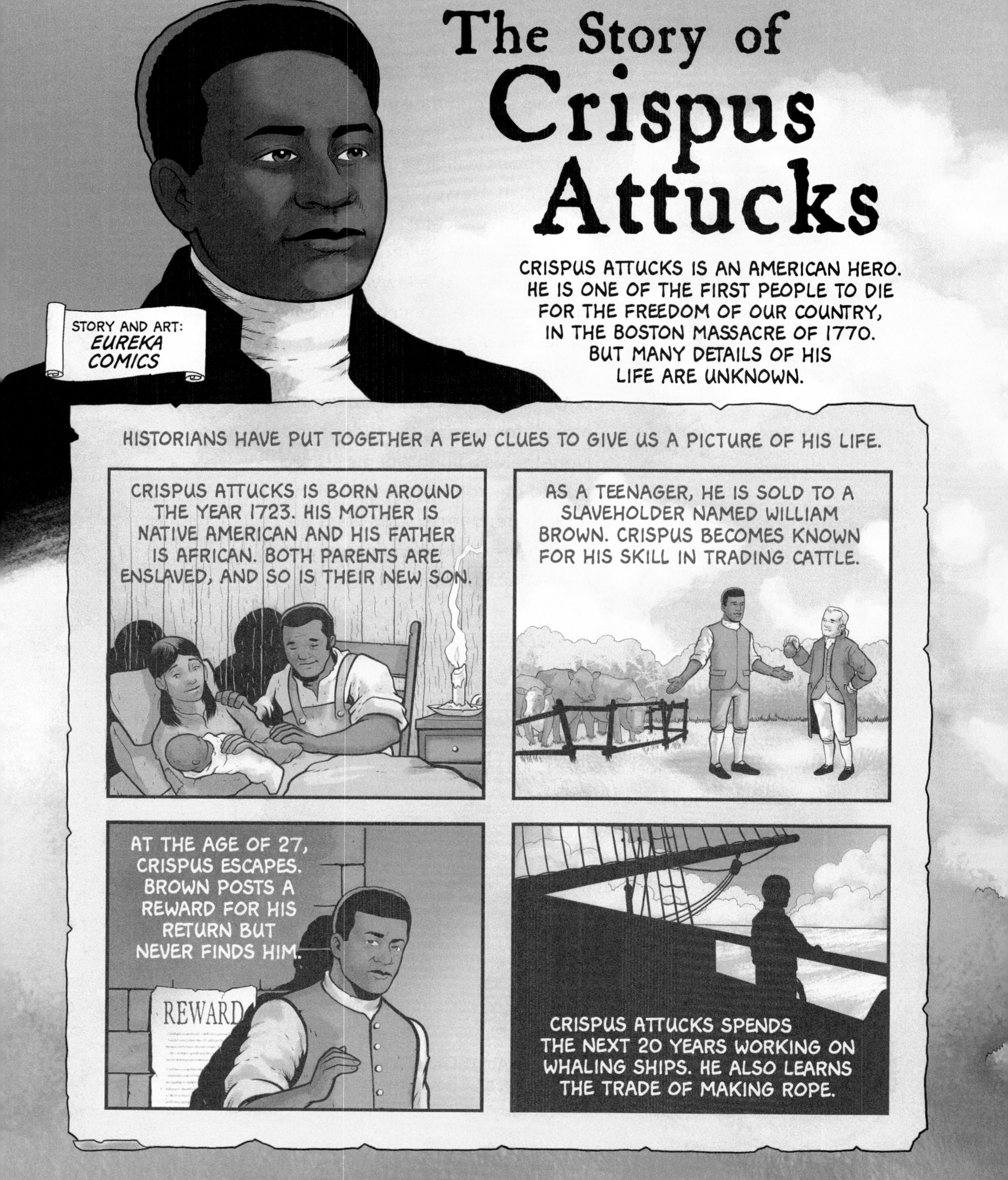
The Story of Crispus Attucks
STORY AND ART: EUREKA COMICS
CRISPUS ATTUCKS IS AN AMERICAN HERO. HE IS ONE OF THE FIRST PEOPLE TO DIE FOR THE FREEDOM OF OUR COUNTRY, IN THE BOSTON MASSACRE OF 1770. BUT MANY DETAILS OF HIS LIFE ARE UNKNOWN.
HISTORIANS HAVE PUT TOGETHER A FEW CLUES TO GIVE US A PICTURE OF HIS LIFE.
CRISPUS ATTUCKS IS BORN AROUND THE YEAR 1723. HIS MOTHER IS NATIVE AMERICAN AND HIS FATHER IS AFRICAN. BOTH PARENTS ARE ENSLAVED, AND SO IS THEIR NEW SON.
AS A TEENAGER, HE IS SOLD TO A SLAVEHOLDER NAMED WILLIAM BROWN. CRISPUS BECOMES KNOWN FOR HIS SKILL IN TRADING CATTLE.
AT THE AGE OF 27, CRISPUS ESCAPES. BROWN POSTS A REWARD FOR HIS RETURN BUT NEVER FINDS HIM.
REWARD
CRISPUS ATTUCKS SPENDS THE NEXT 20 YEARS WORKING ON WHALING SHIPS. HE ALSO LEARNS THE TRADE OF MAKING ROPE.

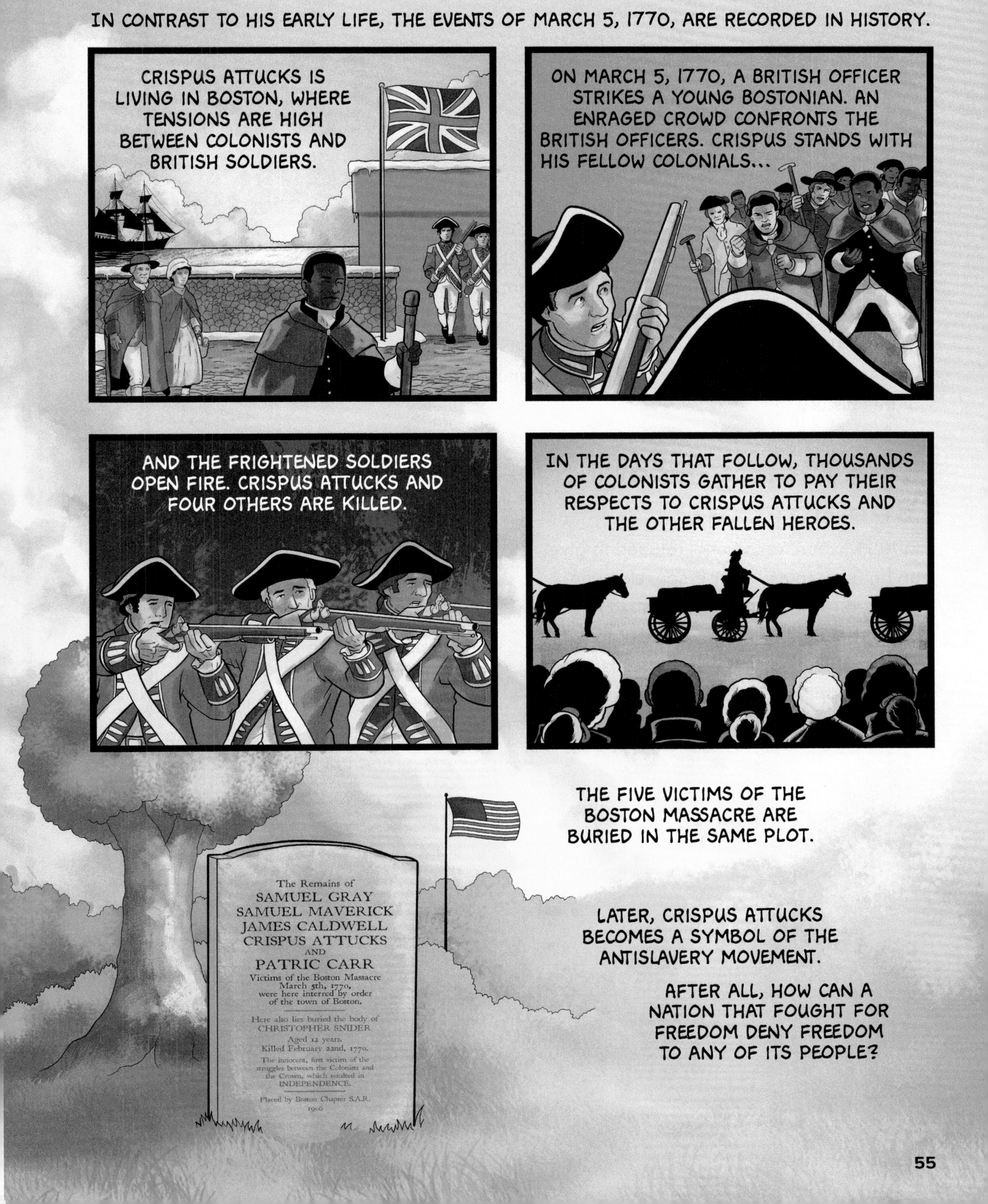
IN CONTRAST TO HIS EARLY LIFE, THE EVENTS OF MARCH 5, 1770, ARE RECORDED IN HISTORY.
CRISPUS ATTUCKS IS LIVING IN BOSTON, WHERE TENSIONS ARE HIGH BETWEEN COLONISTS AND BRITISH SOLDIERS.
ON MARCH 5, 1770, A BRITISH OFFICER STRIKES A YOUNG BOSTONIAN. AN ENRAGED CROWD CONFRONTS THE BRITISH OFFICERS. CRISPUS STANDS WITH HIS FELLOW COLONIALS...
AND THE FRIGHTENED SOLDIERS OPEN FIRE. CRISPUS ATTUCKS AND FOUR OTHERS ARE KILLED.
IN THE DAYS THAT FOLLOW, THOUSANDS OF COLONISTS GATHER TO PAY THEIR RESPECTS TO CRISPUS ATTUCKS AND THE OTHER FALLEN HEROES.
THE FIVE VICTIMS OF THE BOSTON MASSACRE ARE BURIED IN THE SAME PLOT.
The Remains of
SAMUEL GRAY
SAMUEL MAVERICK
JAMES CALDWELL
CRISPUS ATTUCKS
AND
PATRIC CARR
Victims of the Boston Massacre March 5th, 1770, were here interred by order of the town of Boston.
Here also lies buried the body of CHRISTOPHER SNIDER
Aged 12 years.
Killed February 22nd, 1770.
The innocent, first victim of the struggles between the Colonists and the Crown, which resulted in INDEPENDENCE.
Placed by Boston Chapter S.A.R.
1906
LATER, CRISPUS ATTUCKS BECOMES A SYMBOL OF THE ANTISLAVERY MOVEMENT.
AFTER ALL, HOW CAN A NATION THAT FOUGHT FOR FREEDOM DENY FREEDOM TO ANY OF ITS PEOPLE?

Citizenship PERSPECTIVES

Boycott!

When American colonists were forced to pay high taxes on British goods such as tea, they responded with a boycott of British imports. This hurt British businesses, and Parliament was pressured to repeal many of the taxes. People have used boycotts to fight wrongs at other pivotal moments in United States history.

Rosa Parks was at the center of the Montgomery Bus Boycott.

The Montgomery Bus Boycott

In 1955, when Rosa Parks refused to give up her seat to a white person, she was arrested. Civil rights leaders called for a boycott of the bus system in Montgomery, Alabama. The boycott was a success. It rallied support against racial injustice across the United States.

The United Farm Workers' Grape Boycott

Migrant workers picking grapes in California earned very low pay and suffered from poor working conditions. In 1968, César Chávez and the United Farm Workers union called for a worldwide boycott of California grapes. The boycott ended in 1970, when grape growers agreed to improve conditions.

(bkgd)Carolin Sunshine/Shutterstock.com, (insets)Bettmann/Getty Im

Take Action!

More to Explore

Here are more questions that you can research and discuss.

What role did American Indians play in events before the Revolutionary War?

How did other leaders of the American Revolution participate in the struggle for independence?

Find out about another boycott in United States history. What were its goals, and what did it achieve?

WordBlast

- How did the **ferocity** of lacrosse help American Indians?
- How is your generation different from your parents **generation**?
- When was George Washington's life in **jeopardy**?
- In what ways did **revolutionaries** protest British control?

ESSENTIAL QUESTION EQ

Reflect

Why would a nation want to become independent?

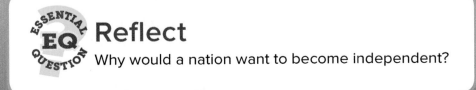

Chapter 5

The American Revolution

ESSENTIAL QUESTION EQ

What does the revolutionary era tell us about our nation today?

Table of Contents

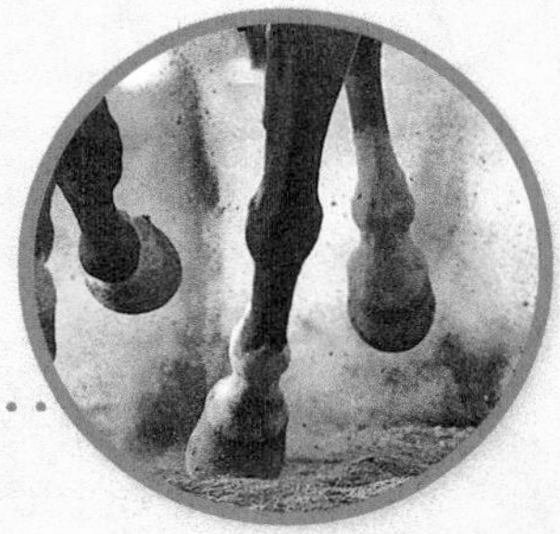

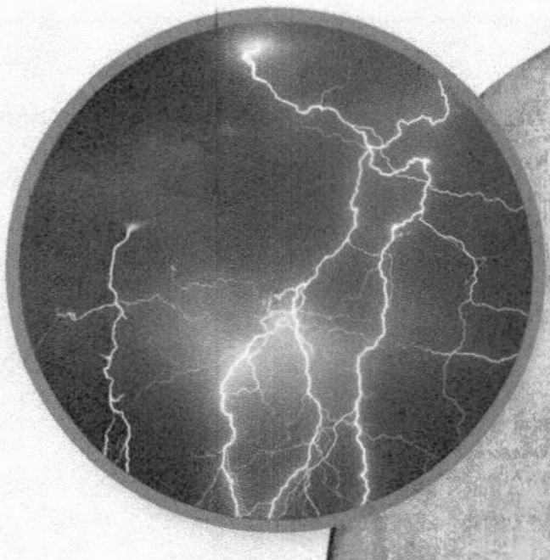

Artifacts of the American Revolution

As this replica shows, a colonial officer's tent was small but allowed the officer some privacy.

This flintlock pistol dates to the Revolutionary War.

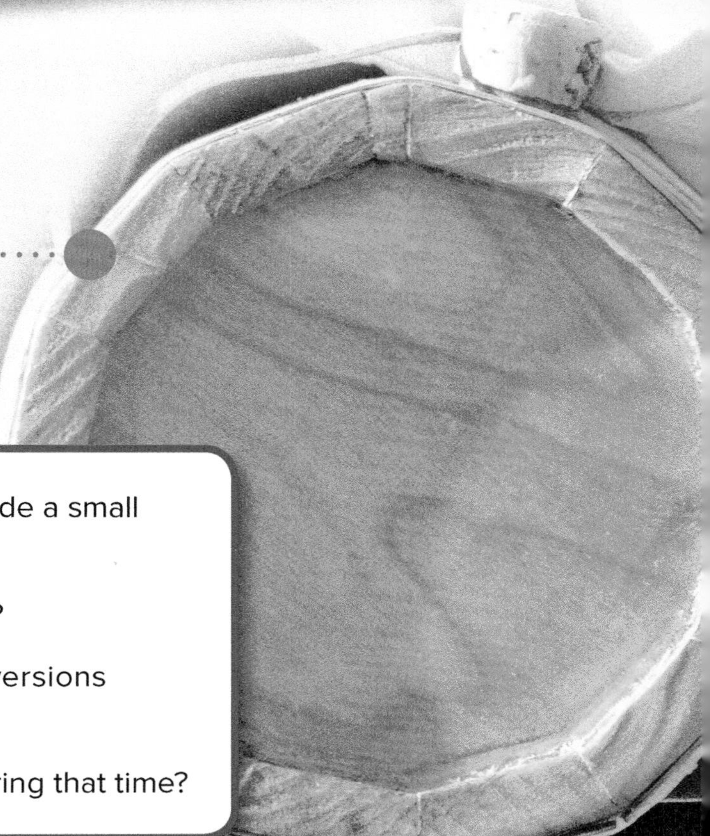

Soldiers used wooden canteens attached to a strap for easy carrying.

These artifacts from the American Revolution provide a small glimpse into life during the war.

- What details do you notice about each artifact?
- How do these artifacts compare with modern versions of these items?
- What can you learn about a soldier's daily life during that time?

Two Midnight Rides

What makes a person legendary? A person is legendary when he or she does something wonderful or brave enough to become famous. Both Sybil Ludington and Paul Revere took legendary rides to help the colonies in their conflict against the British during the American Revolution.

On April 16, 1775, Paul Revere rode his horse to Concord, Massachusetts. He warned the colonial soldiers to protect their supply of weapons from the advancing British troops. On April 18, 1775, Revere rode from Charlestown to Boston to warn soldiers that the British were coming.

Two years later, on the night of April 26, 1777, sixteen-year-old Sybil Ludington rode forty miles on her horse to Danbury, Connecticut. She warned soldiers that the British were coming. Today we can see reminders of Sybil's ride. There is a statue of Sybil on horseback that stands in Carmel, New York, and a postage stamp issued in her honor.

CONNECT THROUGH LITERATURE

Another Spectacular Ride

by **Drollene P. Brown**

This work of historical fiction imagines the night that Sybil Ludington, daughter of Colonel Henry Ludington, notices an unnatural red glow in the east. It is the evening of April 26, 1777. After dinner, a courier arrives at the Ludington home with news.

Turning to Sybil, Colonel Ludington said, "That red glow in the sky is from Danbury, Connecticut. There are about two thousand British soldiers there burning the town, and they're heading for Ridgefield. I must stay here to prepare for the battle, but someone must alert our men."

"I'll go! Star and I can do it!" Sybil exclaimed. Sybil's horse, Star, was sure of foot and would do anything Sybil asked.

"There are dangers other than slippery paths," her mother warned. "Outlaws or deserters or even British soldiers may be on the road. You must be wary in a way that Star cannot."

"I can do it," Sybil declared.

Without another word, Abigail turned to fetch a woolen cape to protect her daughter from the wind and rain. Sybil swung up onto her sturdy horse with a stick in her hand. As though reciting an oath, she repeated her father's directions: "Go south by the river, then along Horse Pound Road to Mahopac Pond. From there, turn right to Red Mills, then go north to Stormville." And then she was off.

Sybil rode up to one cottage after another and beat on each door with her stick. "Look at the sky!" she shouted. "Danbury's burning! All men muster at Ludington's!"

The roads were often slippery with mud and wet stones, and the **terrain** was frequently hilly and wooded. Sybil's ears strained for sounds of other riders who might try to steal her horse or stop her mission. Twice she pulled Star off the path while unknown riders passed within a few feet. By the time they reached Stormville, Sybil's voice was almost gone. But the town's call to arms was sounding as horse and rider turned homeward.

Covered with mud and tired beyond belief, Sybil could barely stay on Star's back as they rode into their own yard close to dawn. She had ridden nearly 40 miles. She had roused several hundred men, and Ludington's regiment marched out to join the Connecticut militia. They helped rout the British at Ridgefield, driving them back to their ships on Long Island Sound.

Afterward, General George Washington gave his personal thanks to Sybil for her courageous deed. Her ride would go down in history, and she would be forever remembered as a heroine of the American Revolution.

WordBlast

What do you think **terrain** means? How does the text help you figure that out?

Washington's Spies

George Washington was a great man. He was president and a general in the American Revolution. But one of the little known facts about him is that he was a spymaster. In fact, during the Revolution, he led a whole spy **network**!

The network was known as the Culper Spy Ring. Benjamin Tallmadge, an officer under Washington, created the network under the general's orders. Also in the group were Robert Townsend, James Rivington, Abraham Woodhull, Austin Roe, Anna Smith Strong, Caleb Brewster, and many others.

Many people gave intelligence and information to the people in the spy ring. From there, the spies sent it to George Washington. But there was a catch to the written messages they sent. Each one was in code, and they used different codes. If any message was intercepted by an enemy who figured out the code, the Spy Ring couldn't apply that code to other written messages.

Sending Secret Messages

Benjamin Tallmadge gave the Culper Spy Ring agents a cipher, shown below. The letters in the bottom row were used in place of the letters in the top row.

WordBlast

What do you think the word **network** means? What are some modern-day ways that networks are formed?

a	b	c	d	e	f	g	h	i	j	k	l	m	n	o	p	q	r	s	t	u	v	w	x	y	z
e	f	g	h	i	j	a	b	c	d	o	m	n	p	q	r	k	l	u	v	w	x	y	z	s	t

George Washington organized a secret spy ring to gather information on British troop movements. His men used invisible ink to hide their messages.

Tallmadge also created a word-number code. The code assigned numbers from 1 to 763 to specific words and names. For example, the number for New York was 727. The number for the word "I" was 280, and the number for "love" was 348. To say "I love New York" in Tallmadge's code, you would use 280-348-727.

The Culper Spy Ring had other codes, and they also used invisible ink. You needed lemon juice to read some messages. Others needed to be heated up. If you needed fire to read a letter, Washington told his agents to put an F in the corner of the letter. If it needed acid, such as lemon juice, Washington told his agents to put an A in the corner of the letter.

Washington's network included people who lived in another country for months, even years, in order to report to him. They knew they risked their lives there, because if they were found out, they would be jailed, sent away, or even killed! We owe a lot to the spies of the American Revolution.

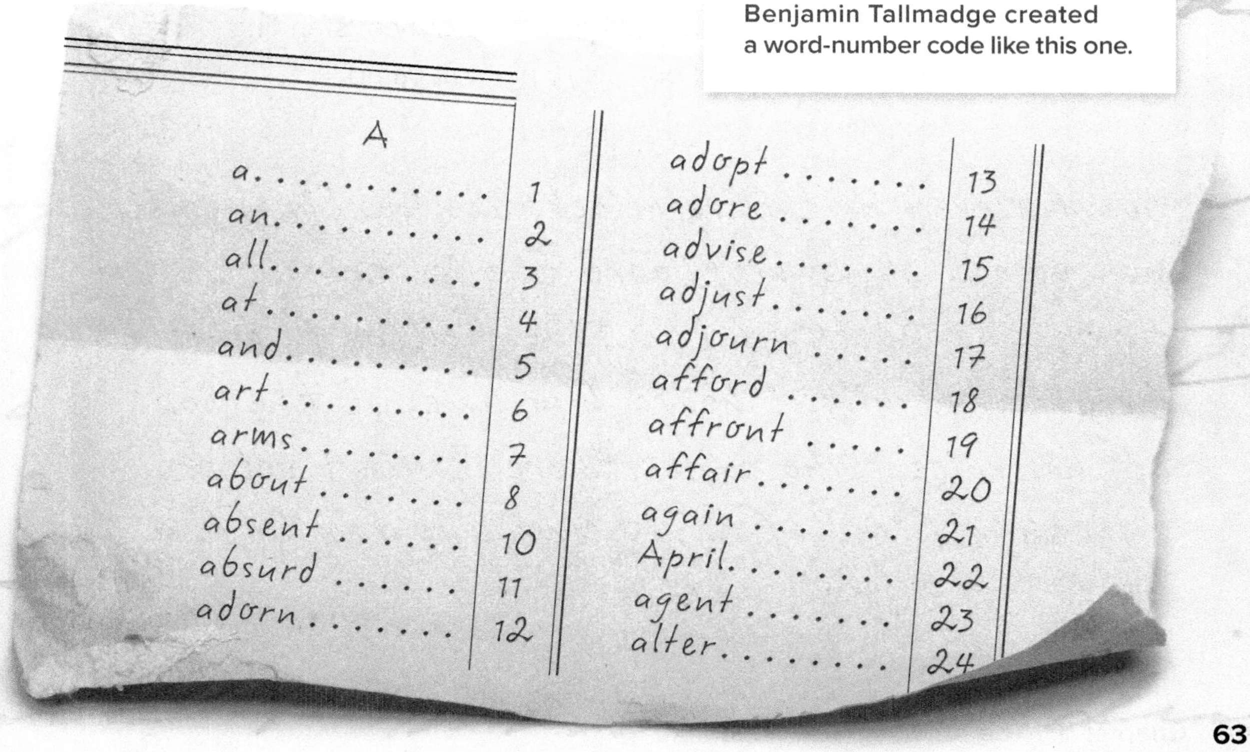

A

a	1	adopt	13
an	2	adore	14
all	3	advise	15
at	4	adjust	16
and	5	adjourn	17
art	6	afford	18
arms	7	affront	19
about	8	affair	20
absent	10	again	21
absurd	11	April	22
adorn	12	agent	23
		alter	24

Benjamin Tallmadge created a word-number code like this one.

Boy Soldier

Going to war is dangerous— too dangerous for youngsters. You must be at least eighteen to join the Army. But during the American Revolution, a few underage soldiers slipped in.

Daniel Granger was only thirteen years old when he first served in the Army. Daniel arrived at the camp of the Continental Army near Boston in November 1775. He intended to pick up his sick older brother and bring him home. Instead, Daniel took his brother's place.

"The Weather was extremely cold," wrote Daniel, when he recorded his memories as an old man. He continued:

> *And Winter Hill was a high bleak & cold place.*

Daniel was issued a musket, and he was given the duty of standing guard overnight. Later he recalled one scary night at camp:

> *About eleven or twelve oclock, the Sentinal that was placed above me, heard the ice trickle down from the Rocks as the Tide fell off, which frightened him, I heard him hale, at the Top of his voice, 'Who comes there' twice I beleave, and then fired off his Gun and ran off.*

Fierman Much/Shutterstock.com

I could hear the Drum beating at the guardhouse to turn out the Guard. I cocked my Gun, looked and lissaned, but could see nor hear anything but the trickling of the Ice on the Shore.

Joining the Army Again

Daniel returned home in the spring to work on the family farm. A year later, young Daniel—now fifteen—again enlisted in the Army. The Army traveled everywhere on foot and was marching across the countryside. They cooked their own food, washed their own clothes, and often slept under the open sky.

Daniel's march of almost 200 miles brought him to Saratoga, New York. The colonial troops "were arranged on both sides of the Road, Drums & Fifes playing Yankee doodle, Cannon roaring in all quarters," Daniel wrote. "The whol World seemed to be in motion."

The Battle of Saratoga was a great American victory. After the excitement, Daniel walked home to Massachusetts. On his way home, he awoke one morning to find himself covered with five or six inches of snow.

About a year later, Daniel again joined the Army—this time as a musician. After the war, Daniel returned to the family farm. Later, he became a teacher, but he never forgot his experience as a boy soldier.

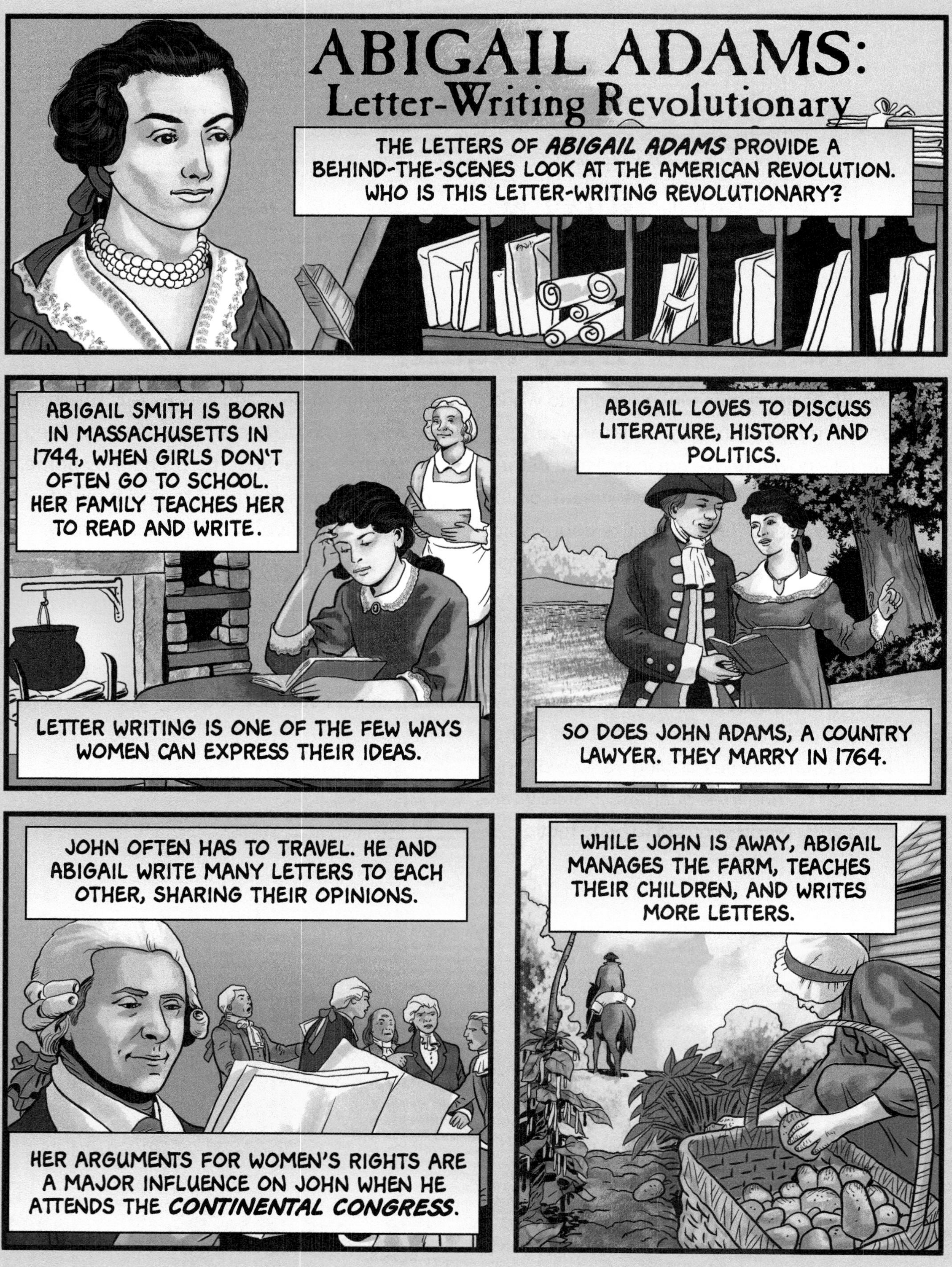
ABIGAIL ADAMS:
Letter-Writing Revolutionary
THE LETTERS OF ABIGAIL ADAMS PROVIDE A BEHIND-THE-SCENES LOOK AT THE AMERICAN REVOLUTION. WHO IS THIS LETTER-WRITING REVOLUTIONARY?
ABIGAIL SMITH IS BORN IN MASSACHUSETTS IN 1744, WHEN GIRLS DON'T OFTEN GO TO SCHOOL. HER FAMILY TEACHES HER TO READ AND WRITE.
LETTER WRITING IS ONE OF THE FEW WAYS WOMEN CAN EXPRESS THEIR IDEAS.
ABIGAIL LOVES TO DISCUSS LITERATURE, HISTORY, AND POLITICS.
SO DOES JOHN ADAMS, A COUNTRY LAWYER. THEY MARRY IN 1764.
JOHN OFTEN HAS TO TRAVEL. HE AND ABIGAIL WRITE MANY LETTERS TO EACH OTHER, SHARING THEIR OPINIONS.
HER ARGUMENTS FOR WOMEN'S RIGHTS ARE A MAJOR INFLUENCE ON JOHN WHEN HE ATTENDS THE CONTINENTAL CONGRESS.
WHILE JOHN IS AWAY, ABIGAIL MANAGES THE FARM, TEACHES THEIR CHILDREN, AND WRITES MORE LETTERS.

ONE MORNING IN 1775, ABIGAIL WAKES UP TO THE SOUND OF CANNON FIRE.
BOOM! BOOM! BOOM!
THE BRITISH ARE MARCHING THROUGH NEARBY CHARLESTOWN, ON THEIR WAY TO THE *BATTLE OF BUNKER HILL*.
ABIGAIL CAN'T EAT OR SLEEP AS THE CANNONS ROAR. SHE WRITES AN ACCOUNT OF THE BATTLE TO HER HUSBAND. SHE SAYS PEOPLE ARE STILL IN GOOD SPIRITS EVEN THOUGH CHARLESTOWN HAS BEEN BURNED TO THE GROUND.
AS WAR RAGES, ABIGAIL GIVES SHELTER TO SOLDIERS, SEWS UNIFORMS, AND MELTS DOWN HER TABLEWARE FOR AMMUNITION.
WHEN PEACE COMES, JOHN IS NAMED AMERICA'S AMBASSADOR TO THE COURTS OF EUROPE. ABIGAIL JOINS HIM IN PARIS.
ABIGAIL CONTINUES TO BE JOHN'S TRUSTED ADVISOR WHEN HE IS ELECTED THE SECOND PRESIDENT OF THE NEW UNITED STATES.
STORY AND ART: *EUREKA COMICS*
TODAY WE REMEMBER HER AS A BRAVE WOMAN WHO USED HER PEN TO CHANGE HEARTS AND MINDS.

A Man of *Many Talents*

Benjamin Franklin

Born in Boston on January 17 — **1706**

Started publishing *Poor Richard's Almanack* — **1733**

Invented the Franklin stove, a fireplace lined in metal that stands in the middle of a room — **1742**

Proposed his famous kite experiment with lightning — **1752**

Served on the committee to write the Declaration of Independence — **1776**

Appointed U.S. Minister to France — **1776**

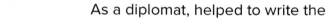

1783 — As a diplomat, helped to write the Treaty of Paris, which brought an end to the American Revolution

1784 — Invented bifocals

1787 — Served as a delegate to the Constitutional Convention

1790 — Died in Philadelphia on April 17

EXPLORE the Timeline

- What does the timeline tell about Benjamin Franklin's interests?
- How does the timeline explain the importance of Benjamin Franklin?
- How old was Benjamin Franklin at key moments of his service to the nation?

Tireless Thinker

Printer. Author. Statesman. Diplomat. Scientist. Inventor. The list of Benjamin Franklin's jobs and accomplishments goes on and on. How did he have time to accomplish so much? He started when he was young.

Born in Boston to Puritan parents in 1706, Franklin attended school only until he was ten years old, but he didn't stop reading and writing. Soon after, he apprenticed at a printing business. Franklin later opened his own printer's shop in Philadelphia where he produced a newspaper and *Poor Richard's Almanack*.

An almanac is a reference book that includes information on topics such as weather forecasts, holidays, and astronomy. Many almanacs, including *Poor Richard's Almanack*, also featured popular sayings, jokes, and proverbs. Ben Franklin wrote many popular sayings that reflected his sense of humor.

He devoted time to his community in Philadelphia and would eventually start a library, a hospital, and the colonial postal system. Franklin also helped start what would become the University of Pennsylvania and the first fire department. He would go on to invent the Franklin stove, bifocals, and an instrument called the glass armonica (pictured above).

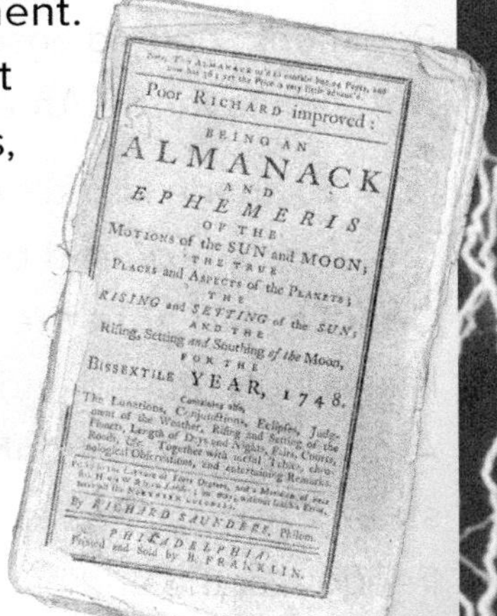

PRIMARY SOURCE

In Their Words...

Benjamin Franklin used *Poor Richard's Almanack* as a place to record his aphorisms, or sayings. Below are some of his sayings. What do they mean?

"Well done, is twice done."

"He that is of opinion money will do everything may well be suspected of doing everything for money."

"One today is worth two tomorrows."

"Employ thy time well, if thou meanest to gain leisure."

"Fish and visitors stink in three days."

TEXT: Franklin, Benjamin. Poor Richard's Almanack. Waterloo, IA: U.S.C. Publishing Co., 1914.; PHOTO: (t)JOE KLAMAR/AFP/Getty Images, (b)Library of Congress Prints and Photographs Division [LC-USZ62-75475]

Citizenship

Remembering

The First Rhode Island Regiment

A Revolutionary War re-enactor poses as a First Rhode Island Regiment soldier in 2003.

During the American Revolution, one regiment was made up mostly of African Americans. The First Rhode Island Regiment, also known as "The Black Regiment," helped ensure the success of the Americans in the American Revolution.

In 1778, Rhode Island had trouble recruiting the troops required by the Continental Congress to fight the British. The Rhode Island legislature decided to have enslaved African Americans fight in the war for the state. These men would be given their freedom at the end of the war. Slave owners received money for any enslaved men who became soldiers.

The new First Rhode Island Regiment, which also included free African Americans, whites, and Narragansett Indians, soon grew to 225 men. The regiment first faced combat at the Battle of Rhode Island in August of 1778, fighting back three attacks by the British. After the battle, the regiment was praised for its role by the American commander, General John Sullivan.

In 1781, this regiment united with the Second Rhode Island Regiment to fight at the Battle of Yorktown, the final battle that led to the end of the American Revolution. On December 25, 1783, the regiment was dissolved at Saratoga, New York. Today, the names of those soldiers are **engraved** on a granite monument in Portsmouth, Rhode Island.

WordBlast

What is the meaning of **engraved?** What might be engraved on the outside of your school?

Take Action!

More to Explore

What else do you want to learn about the American Revolution? Here are some questions to guide your research and discussion.

Paul Revere was one of several riders who warned the Patriots of the British patrols. Two others were William Dawes and Samuel Prescott. Find out more about them.

Write a message to George Washington using the Culper cipher found on page 62.

Find out more about Benjamin Franklin. What do you think were his most interesting contributions to modern American life?

WordBlast

- Find a monument in your town. What words are **engraved** on it?
- What are the advantages of using a **network** to accomplish a complex task?
- How did the **terrain** add to the difficulty of Sybil Ludington's ride?

ESSENTIAL QUESTION EQ

Reflect

What does the revolutionary era tell us about our nation today?

Chapter 6

Forming a New Government

How does the Constitution help us understand what it means to be an American?

Table of Contents

Signing the Constitution

Howard Chandler Christy painted "Scene at the Signing of the Constitution of the United States" in 1939, many years after the event it depicts.

Before painting this scene, the artist studied many historic portraits of the signers of the Constitution.

- How would you characterize George Washington, the leader of the Convention, based on the painter's portrayal?
- What message do you think the artist wants to express about the signing of the Constitution? How do you know?

A Place Where Dreams Come True

by **Carolyn Gard**

A Journey to the Northwest Territory

The following account is a personal history of the Dunsmoor family's journey west. Ataline Dunsmoor Gard is the author's great-great-grandmother by marriage.

Phineas Dunsmoor was a lucky man: He and his wife had five sons and two daughters. He owned a tavern in New Hampshire and three hundred acres of farmland. Yet he dreamed of having enough land so that each of his children could have a farm of his or her own someday.

Travelers to his tavern told Dunsmoor about the Northwest Territory, where a person could buy many acres of land at a reasonable price. He decided to move his family west in the hope of fulfilling his dream of a secure future for his children.

The family packed their possessions into two horse-drawn covered wagons. The seven Dunsmoor children—Horace, Abner, Mary, Hiel, Lucius, Ataline, and Daniel—set off with their parents for the Northwest Territory in May 1822.

Two and a half months after leaving New Hampshire, the family arrived in Wesley Township, Ohio, on the Ohio River. Dunsmoor had traded his tavern and land in New Hampshire to a man from the Ohio Company of Associates, the company that first settled present-day Ohio. In the trade, Dunsmoor received nine hundred acres of land on Goose Creek near the town.

Clearing land for a home in the Northwest Territory required hard work by the entire family.

Starting a New Life

The family could not move onto the new property right away. They lived in the town schoolhouse while Dunsmoor and his sons cleared the forest. At that time, clearing an acre of land—approximately the size of a football field—usually took one person about three weeks. Dunsmoor hauled the logs six miles to a mill, where they were sawed into lumber to be used for the family's two-story farmhouse.

One day in the spring of 1823, tragedy struck. Dunsmoor became sick and died a week later. But he had achieved his dream: Each child would have enough land for his or her own farm.

The family **persevered**. They planted and tended fields of corn and grain. When the grain was harvested, they carried it six miles to a grist mill. Then they carried the coarsely ground grain twenty miles to Marietta, Ohio, to be sold.

The Northwest Territory offered many opportunities for hard-working people to succeed, and the Dunsmoors did just that. Among the jobs the family members held over the years were justice of the peace, township treasurer, trustee, assessor, schoolteacher, and county commissioner.

The Dunsmoors, like many others, moved to the Northwest Territory in search of a better life. And the West offered that.

WordBlast

What is the meaning of **persevered**? In what ways did the family persevere?

Your Life as a Farmer

Neighbors and extended family members formed a close community on eastern farms in the 1700s.

In 1787, a group of about 1500 men led by Revolutionary War veteran Daniel Shays attempted to overthrow the government. In an event known as Shays's Rebellion, the men tried to seize weapons at a federal armory in Springfield, Massachusetts. What would motivate these Americans to rebel against their own government?

Imagine you were a farmer in Massachusetts before the Revolutionary War. Earlier settlers were already farming on the most fertile land, near the Connecticut River. Before the war, your life was filled with hard work. You **cultivated** only part of your large tract of land because farming took much time and energy. In such an isolated region, it was difficult to find workers to plant and harvest your crops.

Fortunately, you, your family, and your neighbors helped one another sow fields and gather crops. Families and friends developed strong ties, coming together for events such as log-rolling, quilting, and barn raisings.

WordBlast

Cultivated originally comes from a Latin word meaning "to till or prepare." How does the surrounding text confirm the meaning of this word?

You grew most of your own food and got water from a well or nearby spring or brook. You used surpluses to obtain goods that you could not produce, such as salt.

You might **barter** for goods and services instead of exchanging cash. For example, in exchange for medical treatment, a blacksmith might shoe a doctor's horse. Or you might trade two bushels of corn for one bushel of wheat from another farm. You can make money from logging, weaving flax, or raising livestock. But the goods from these activities are transported over rutted roads or on the Connecticut River. It takes a long time to receive payment.

Life was good before the Revolutionary War, but harsh after the war. You returned from the fighting to find that your family had difficulty producing necessities in your absence. Without surpluses, you must eventually claim bankruptcy and mortgage your farm. Part of your financial problem stems from your isolation from the large eastern commerce centers. Coastal city dwellers, including merchants and shippers, were more fortunate because their trade with other colonies continued during the war.

You become frustrated when facing businessmen focused on cash transactions and profits. You are forced to sell horses, plows, and livestock, often for less than their value, to pay your debts. You need these assets to farm, but you are threatened with jail if you do not pay what you owe. If you are jailed, you cannot earn money to improve your situation. How can you make the government understand how difficult your circumstances are?

WordBlast

Barter means "to exchange goods without using money." Could bartering work in today's world? Why or why not?

Farmers in Massachusetts raised livestock and crops such as corn and wheat.

At the Constitutional Convention

Illustrations by Chris Ware

The U.S. Constitution is the oldest written constitution in existence.

Despite the summer heat, the delegates worked secretly behind closed windows and doors. Guards were even posted outside the doors of the Pennsylvania State House to prevent spies and curious citizens from disturbing the men.

Except for speaking once at the signing of the Constitution, Pennsylvania delegate Jared Ingersoll did not address the group or participate in debates during the entire four months of the convention.

Philadelphia's leaders had the cobblestone streets covered with dirt so that the delegates would not be disturbed by the sound of horses and carriages clattering along outside the State House.

Only thirty-eight delegates actually signed the Constitution on September 17, 1787. Fourteen delegates had returned to their homes before signing began. Three delegates chose not to sign. John Dickinson was absent when the signing took place, but his name does appear on the document (making thirty-nine signatures). He asked his fellow delegate from Delaware, George Read, to sign for him.

DOES ANYBODY KNOW HOW TO SPELL 'Dickinson'?

BOOM!
no, thanks!
R.I.

Suspecting that the Constitutional Convention was going to attempt to overthrow the current government, Rhode Island did not send any delegates.

A Home *for the* Constitution

The Constitution is one of our nation's key documents. Where have the four parchment pages containing the original Constitution resided for the last 230-plus years?

1787

After nearly four months of passionate debate, the Constitutional Convention adjourns. The Convention secretary delivers a signed copy of the Constitution to the secretary of the Continental Congress.

1789

The original Declaration of Independence and Constitution, written on parchment (paper made of animal skin), are probably kept rolled up. The State Department becomes responsible for these and other records and documents.

1814

As the British advance on Washington during the War of 1812, government workers flee with important materials. But they leave the Declaration of Independence and Constitution behind! A State Department clerk puts them in linen bags and takes them by wagon to Leesburg, Virginia. The British later set fire to many parts of Washington, D.C.

This engraving shows George Washington making a speech at the Constitutional Convention.

1814–1921

The Constitution is kept at the State Department.

1921

President Warren G. Harding asks Congress to preserve and exhibit the Declaration of Independence and the Constitution by transferring them to the Library of Congress.

1941–1945 (World War II)

The Declaration of Independence and the Constitution are sent to Fort Knox, Kentucky, for safekeeping. This is one of the country's most secure sites, where the nation's gold reserves are stored.

December 31, 1952
A military escort accompanies the Declaration of Independence and the Constitution as they are moved to the National Archives building in Washington, D.C.

1952–Today
The public can view the Constitution, the Declaration of Independence, and the Bill of Rights. They are displayed in airtight cases in the National Archives Exhibition Hall.

EXPLORE the Timeline

Use the timeline to answer these questions.

- When was the Constitution in danger of being stolen or burnt?
- After being saved during the War of 1812, how long was the Constitution kept at the State Department?
- Why was the Constitution kept at Fort Knox?
- In what city can you see the Constitution today?

Citizenship PERSPECTIVES

Age Appropriate

Electing our leaders and running for office are two of our most important constitutional rights. But not all citizens enjoy these rights equally. For example, you have to be at least eighteen years old to vote. To serve in the House of Representatives, you must be twenty-five; to serve in the Senate, it's thirty. And you have to be at least thirty-five years old to be president.

The Constitution originally gave the states the right to determine the minimum voting age. But during World War II, the age that men were drafted into the military was lowered to eighteen. Many Americans believed that if people were old enough to fight in a war, they were old enough to vote. In the 1960s, the debate became more intense when many young people fought in the Vietnam War. The 26th Amendment to the Constitution was **ratified** in 1971. It established a national voting age of eighteen.

Some teenagers argue that if they are old enough to vote and to serve in the armed forces, why aren't they eligible to serve in Congress? After all, that's where the decisions about whether or not to go to war are made!

What do you think? Does the Constitution grant second-class citizenship to younger Americans? And who should decide these issues—the federal government or state governments?

WordBlast

What does **ratified** mean? How does the text help you figure that out?

Take Action!

More to Explore

What else would you like to learn about? The following questions can help guide your research and discussion.

What types of roads and forms of transportation were used by Northwest Territory settlers?

How did the Bill of Rights become part of the Constitution?

Who are some of the youngest Americans to serve in Congress and as president?

WordBlast

- Why did eighteenth-century farmers often **barter** in order to obtain goods?
- What methods do twenty-first-century farmers use to **cultivate** their land?
- Describe a time when you or someone you know **persevered**.
- What happens when an amendment to the United States Constitution is **ratified?**

ESSENTIAL QUESTION EQ

Reflect

How does the Constitution help us understand what it means to be an American?

Chapter 7

Life in the Young Republic

ESSENTIAL QUESTION EQ

How were the early years of the United States transformative for the nation?

Table of Contents

Invention, Innovation, and Inspiration

Steam locomotives on the transcontinental railroad made it possible for countless Americans to head west.

Steamboats turned waterways into a fast route for moving passengers and cargo.

The Erie Canal connected the Great Lakes to the New York City area. Barges pulled by mules held more cargo than wagons and lowered the cost of shipping goods for businesses.

These pictures show different innovations that changed transportation in the early years of the United States.

- Why were these innovations important to the growth of the United States?
- Why did inventors rely on steam to power locomotives and steamboats?
- How did the Erie Canal help businesses grow?

MEASURE OF A MAN: BENJAMIN BANNEKER

Ellicott's Task

In 1790, Major Andrew Ellicott received an important assignment from the new president, George Washington. President Washington appointed Major Ellicott to measure and survey a ten-mile square by the Potomac River for the new national capital.

Ellicott needed an assistant who could use the complicated tools needed for land surveys. Few people were skilled enough to use these instruments, and nearly all of them were busy with projects of their own. There was one person who could do the job: Benjamin Banneker.

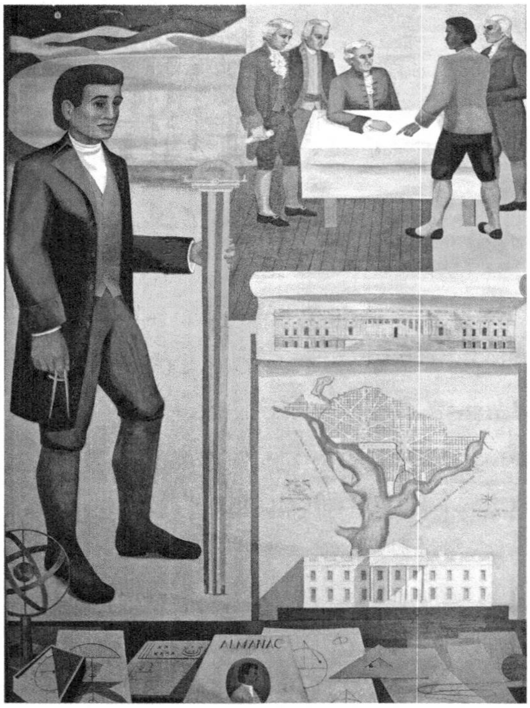

Benjamin Banneker and Andrew Ellicott used tools to survey the land. Today's surveyors still measure and map the geographical features of a piece of land before any construction is done.

Banneker's Life

Benjamin Banneker was born a free African American at Ellicott's Mills in Baltimore County, Maryland, in 1731. He worked on his family's farm, which included a vegetable garden, fruit orchards, and beehives. Banneker had very little formal education, but he taught himself to read. He also learned math on his own and liked to make and solve math puzzles for fun.

When Banneker was fifty-eight years old, he taught himself astronomy—the study of stars and planets. He often borrowed books on astronomy from his neighbor, George Ellicott. When Andrew Ellicott came to ask his cousin George for help with the survey, George recommended Banneker.

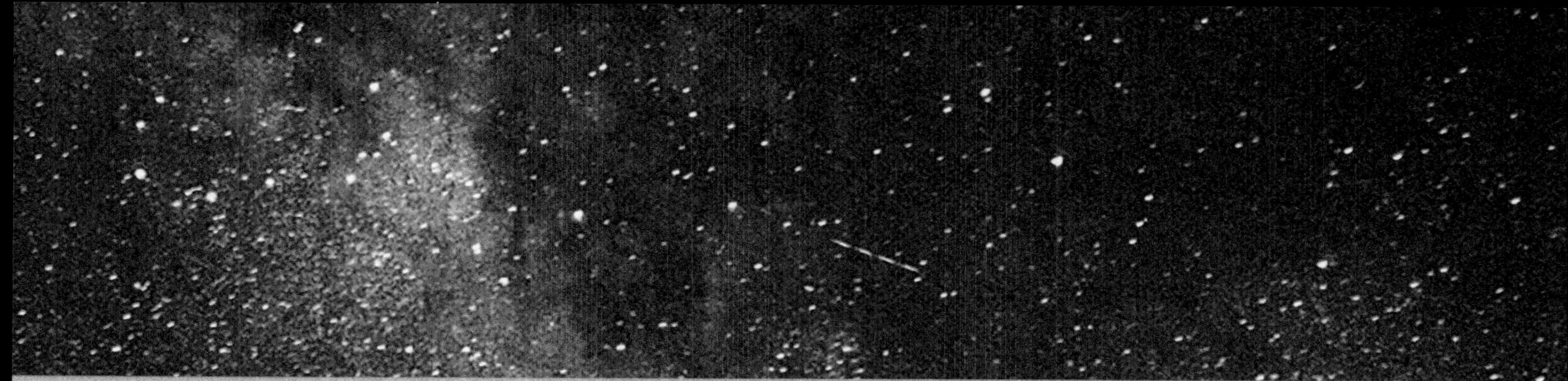

A Job Well Done

Banneker began his work in early February 1791. Every night for the next three months, he would lie on the cold, hard ground in an unheated field observatory tent and look up through a six-foot-long telescope. He then wrote his observations in a book for Ellicott to use the next day. His calculations were used to establish significant points in the nation's capital. Although the job was difficult, he was proud to contribute to such an important project and to learn so much about astronomy.

Writing Almanacs

Banneker spent his days working on special calculations for an almanac. Almanacs were popular informational books long ago that people used for weather forecasts and predicting the movement of the planets. Banneker's almanacs included information about the weather and ocean tides, as well as medical advice and opinion pieces.

Banneker was called the "first African American man of science" because he successfully taught himself mathematics, astronomy, and the use of the most advanced astronomical tools of his time.

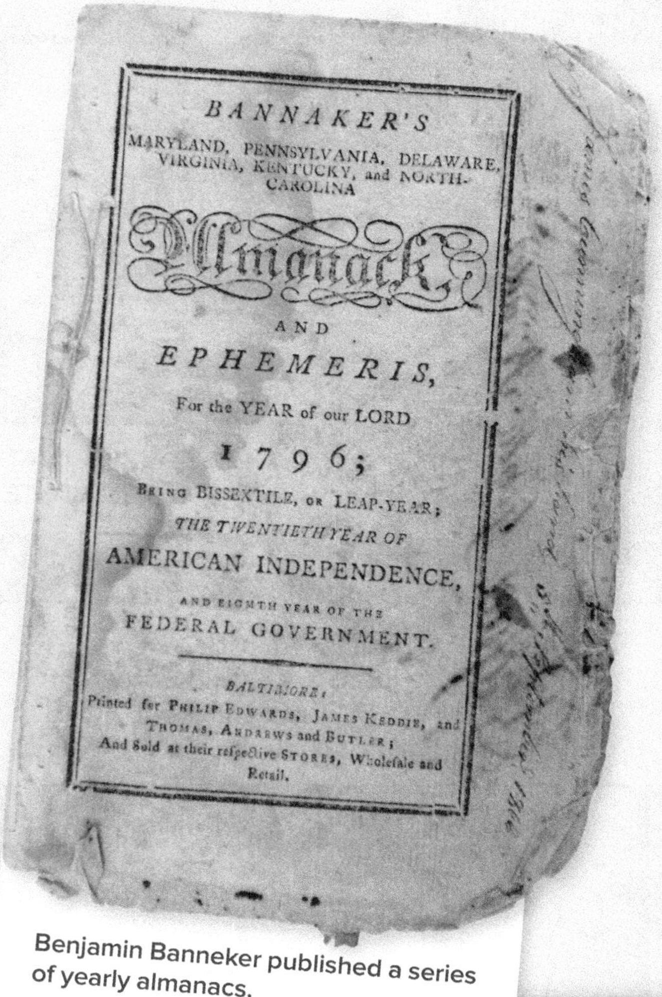
BANNAKER'S
MARYLAND, PENNSYLVANIA, DELAWARE, VIRGINIA, KENTUCKY, and NORTH-CAROLINA
Almanack,
AND
EPHEMERIS,
For the YEAR of our LORD
1796;
BEING BISSEXTILE, OR LEAP-YEAR;
THE TWENTIETH YEAR OF
AMERICAN INDEPENDENCE,
AND EIGHTH YEAR OF THE
FEDERAL GOVERNMENT.
BALTIMORE:
Printed for PHILIP EDWARDS, JAMES KEDDIE, and THOMAS, ANDREWS and BUTLER; And Sold at their respective STORES, Wholesale and Retail.

Benjamin Banneker published a series of yearly almanacs.

Alexander Hamilton

ALEXANDER HAMILTON IS BORN IN THE MID-1750S IN THE BRITISH WEST INDIES.
HE IS RAISED BY A SINGLE MOTHER. SHE PASSES AWAY WHILE HE IS STILL A BOY.
STORY AND ART: EUREKA COMICS
AS A TEENAGER, ALEXANDER WORKS AS A CLERK FOR AN IMPORT BUSINESS.
HE REALIZES THAT HE LIKES TO WRITE.
ONE OF HIS ESSAYS IS PUBLISHED IN THE NEWSPAPER. PEOPLE IN HIS COMMUNITY ARE IMPRESSED. THEY RAISE MONEY AND SEND HIM AWAY TO COLLEGE IN THE AMERICAN COLONIES.
IN 1773, HE ENROLLS AT KING'S COLLEGE IN NEW YORK. HE IS QUICKLY SWEPT UP IN THE COLONISTS' REBELLION AGAINST BRITISH RULE.
HE LENDS HIS WRITING AND SPEAKING TALENTS TO THE CAUSE.
AS THE AMERICAN REVOLUTION BEGINS, HAMILTON'S WORDS GIVE WAY TO ACTION.
IN 1775, HE BECOMES A SOLDIER IN THE FIGHT FOR AMERICAN INDEPENDENCE.

SERVING UNDER GENERAL WASHINGTON, HAMILTON LEADS TROOPS AT YORKTOWN, VIRGINIA. THE VICTORY WINS THE WAR FOR THE AMERICANS.
AFTER THE WAR, HAMILTON HELPS SHAPE AMERICA'S NEW GOVERNMENT. HE SERVES AS A DELEGATE TO THE CONSTITUTIONAL CONVENTION.
AS THE FIRST TREASURY SECRETARY OF THE UNITED STATES AND AN OPINIONATED POLITICIAN, HAMILTON MAKES ENEMIES. CHIEF AMONG THEM: VICE PRESIDENT AARON BURR.
IN 1804, BURR CHALLENGES HAMILTON TO A DUEL. ON THE MORNING OF JULY 11, THE TWO MEN MEET. WHEN THEY FIRE THEIR PISTOLS, HAMILTON'S SHOT MISSES. BURR'S DOES NOT.
ALEXANDER HAMILTON DIES THE NEXT DAY.
RESERVE NOTE
10
FEDERAL
10
WE REMEMBER HIM AS ONE OF THE FOUNDERS OF OUR NATION. HE HELPS CREATE THE U.S. MINT, THE FIRST NATIONAL BANK, AND THE U.S. COAST GUARD.
THOUGH HIS LIFE IS CUT SHORT, ALEXANDER HAMILTON HAS A LASTING INFLUENCE ON OUR COUNTRY. THAT'S WHY WE SEE HIM ON OUR $10 BILLS!
10
TEN
HAMILTON

Lewis and Clark: *Wildlife Adventures*

Imagine what it would be like to set foot in an entirely new land. All that lies before you is unknown. Each step you take is one that places you further from home, but deeper into a world full of plants and animals you have never seen before. One famous duo, Meriwether Lewis and William Clark, faced the reality of venturing across an unknown land. This land was the American West, home to all kinds of undiscovered wildlife. President Jefferson commissioned the two men to carry out an expedition to explore Western lands.

Almost a year into their travels, Lewis and Clark—leaders of the Corps of Discovery—sent back about a dozen men to report to President Thomas Jefferson. These men delivered Lewis and Clark's written reports about what the Corps of Discovery had seen on the journey so far. The men carried maps, animal skins and skeletons, and many samples of plants and rocks. They even brought along five live animals, including a prairie dog that would eventually live with President Jefferson at the White House.

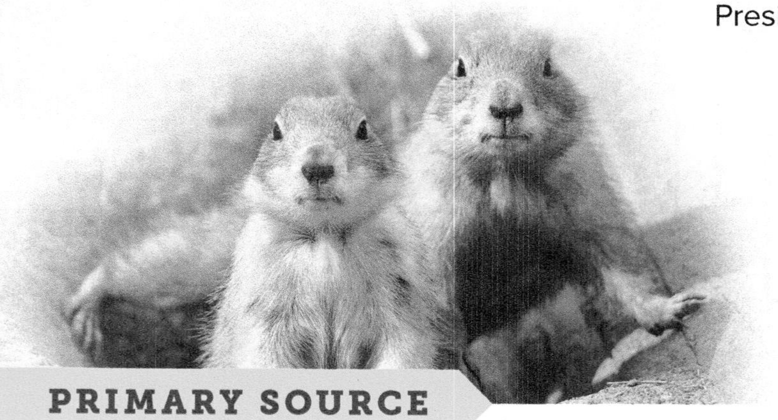

Prairie dogs fascinated Lewis and Clark so much that they gave one to President Jefferson.

PRIMARY SOURCE

In Their Words...

. . . . the Village of those animals . . . . Contains great numbers of holes on the top of which those little animals Set erect, make a Whistleing noise and whin allarmed Slip into their hole . . . . about the Size of a Small Squ[ir]rel . . . . except the ears which is Shorter, his tail like a ground squir[r]el which they shake & whistle when allarmd.

—written by **William Clark** on September 7, 1804, after seeing prairie dogs for the first time

As they crossed most of present-day Montana, the Americans were amazed by the wildlife they saw. They already had come upon many "new" animals such as antelope and coyotes. Now they reported seeing herds of buffalo numbering in the tens of thousands. They wrote about their encounters with the deadliest animal they would face along their journey: the grizzly bear, which they called the "White Bear" or "Yellow Bear." The grizzly bear showed the Corps of Discovery just how **treacherous** the American West could be. The group fought off several grizzly bear attacks over the course of their travels.

Lewis and Clark saw the Great Falls of the Missouri River as a beautiful yet troublesome sight.

Despite the dangers they faced, the expedition continued westward. In June of 1805, the explorers reached the Great Falls of the Missouri River. The sight was breathtaking, but it was not welcome. The travelers would have to get around the falls by land. That meant transporting their equipment and supplies for about eighteen miles! It took them almost an entire month.

Lewis and Clark overcame the harsh terrain to arrive at the Pacific Ocean. Over the course of their historic journey, they discovered at least 120 animal species and 180 plant species.

WordBlast

Treacherous means "full of danger or treachery." What treacherous things or places did Lewis and Clark encounter on their expedition?

Buffalo were a common sight for Lewis and Clark.

(bkgd spread)Ruslan74/Shutterstock.com; (t)David R. Frazier/Danita Delimont Photography/Newscom; (c)Tim Zurowski/Shutterstock.com; (b)Randy Beacham/Alamy Stock Photo

THE TRANSCONTINENTAL RAILROAD

Long ago, traveling from the East to California was nearly impossible. Then Congress passed the Pacific Railroad Act of 1862 so that a railroad could be built to connect the East and the West. In 1863, the Central Pacific Railroad Company began laying tracks heading east from Sacramento. The Union Pacific Railroad Company would lay tracks west from the Missouri River. Both companies raced to see who could lay the most miles of track before they met in the middle.

Workers wave as a Central Pacific Railroad train comes out of a snow-covered tunnel.

Work was difficult. Everything had to be done by hand—shoveling dirt, blasting rock, hammering spikes, and hauling lumber. Charles Crocker, the head of construction for Central Pacific, could not keep workers from quitting. Someone suggested that he hire Chinese immigrants.

At first, he hired fifty Chinese workers. They worked hard and learned quickly. **Eventually,** thousands more Chinese immigrants were hired. Some were brought directly from China. Although they were excellent workers, their pay was not good. The Chinese workers had to cook their own food and live in the rock tunnels they were constructing. The Chinese managed to stay healthier than the other workers by bathing often, washing their clothes, and drinking tea made with boiled water.

On May 10, 1869, the two railroads met at Promontory Summit, Utah. The Central Pacific workers had laid 690 miles of track, and the Union Pacific had laid track for 1,087 miles. Now travelers from the East could easily reach California in one week instead of several months.

WordBlast

Eventually means "at a later time, in the end." What eventually happened because of the transcontinental railroad?

Workers build a track bed through a ravine about 82 miles from Sacramento.

CONNECT THROUGH LITERATURE

from Working on the Railroad

by **Howard Gutner**

Li Ho unwrapped his leather pack and took out his pen and paper. The sun already was burning the back of his neck, so he knew it would be another hot day.

He neatly folded a piece of paper and squinted into the sun. Lines of horses and mules were standing near the camp train getting their daily breakfast of hay and barley.

Li tried to focus his thoughts, as he had only a few moments to write a short note to his wife, Xue-li (SOO lee), back in San Francisco. He chewed on the tip of his pencil before he began to write.

August 1866

Dear Xue-li,

Today we continue to clear a level roadbed for the railroad track. It seems to be the only work that we Chinese workers have done here. Each day is the same—the same hard work, the same hot weather.

Good news: We have received a raise, from $30 to $35 a month! After I buy food and other articles here, I should be able to send you $20 a month in gold. I now know we made the right decision to come to America. There are so many opportunities for us to have a better life here. The wages are much higher than in China, and if I keep working hard, I'm certain we will have some land of our own and a nice home soon!

I must go now. Kiss our beautiful daughter for me.

Love,

Li

The Era of

GOOD FEELINGS

This bronze peace medal with a profile of Monroe is engraved with the words "Peace and Friendship."

For a country with "United" in its name, the United States has certainly had its problems staying whole. When James Monroe became president, he hoped to stop the growing divide between the states. The "Era of Good Feelings," a popular description of Monroe's early presidency, resulted from his efforts to encourage national harmony. Monroe took on the challenge of keeping the United States united one mile at a time—*literally.*

Shortly after his 1817 inauguration, Monroe announced his plan to go on a tour. He hoped that his tour would end fighting among the country's political **factions.** Monroe did not believe that political parties were necessary, and he wanted to heal the split between Federalists and Republicans.

At first, Monroe tried to travel without attracting attention. He went to Baltimore, Maryland, with only a few officials in his carriage. However, when he arrived there on Sunday, June 1, he was met by cavalry units and cheering crowds.

Following his stop in Baltimore, Maryland, Monroe traveled through cities in the East, including New York City. Monroe's visit to Boston for Fourth of July celebrations was the most important stop on his tour. As he rode horseback through the city, thousands of people lined the streets.

President Monroe went on to make several more stops on his way to Detroit, where he began his journey back home. Every town on the tour gave the president a hearty welcome, and Monroe did his best to be enthusiastic. By the time he returned to Washington, D.C., in September, Monroe was exhausted. Nevertheless, he chose to take another tour in 1819.

His second tour came at a time in which the country was in an economic depression and, once again, divided. Unfortunately, his second tour did not receive the same enthusiasm as his first, and the "Era of Good Feelings" did not last into his second term as president. However, Monroe did, for a time, help unify the country.

WordBlast

What is the meaning of **factions?** What two factions are mentioned in the text?

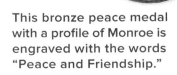

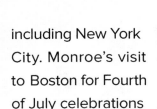

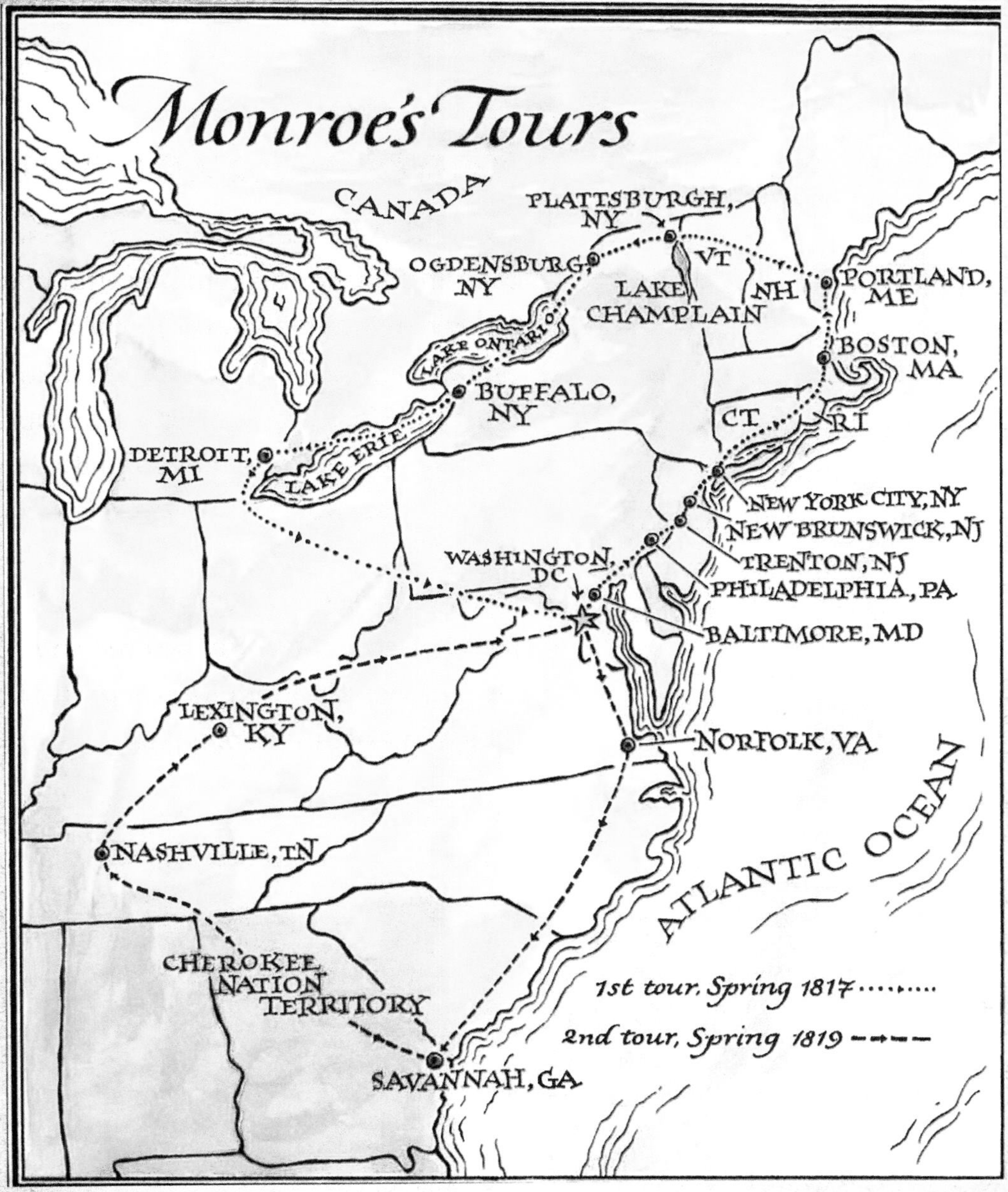

EXPLORE the Map

With a partner, look closely at the map.

- Which of the Great Lakes did Monroe cross?
- Monroe crossed through the territory of which American Indian nation?
- Why do you think Monroe went to the cities he did?

What are some questions you have about the map? With your partner, figure out how you could find answers to these questions.

Coming to America

What would it be like to leave everything—your friends, family, and home—behind to start over in a new country? Perhaps you already know what that is like, or maybe your parents, grandparents, or great-grandparents know. The chances are that somewhere along the way, one or more of your ancestors entered the United States as an immigrant. Their struggles and the struggles of newcomers from other countries today show the real strength of Americans.

Years of Expansion

After the American colonies had claimed their independence, immigrants played a key role in the expansion of the United States. During the California Gold Rush of the mid-1800s, many people from Northern and Western Europe moved to the United States to escape war, poverty, and hunger. However, their new life here was not easy. Many Catholics, especially the Irish Catholics, faced discrimination for their religious beliefs. Others viewed them as competition for jobs and treated them unfairly.

An immigrant family looks at the New York City skyline.

Jane Addams helped improve the lives of immigrants at the Hull House in Chicago, Illinois.

(bkgd)Agnieszka Szymczak/E+/Getty Images, (insets)Bettmann/Getty Images

Jane Addams worked to make immigrants' lives better.

The Immigration Boom

Between the late 1800s and mid-1900s, immigration to the United States skyrocketed. People from all over the world poured into the country. They often came in search of wealth, especially during times like the California Gold Rush. Just as others before them, newcomers during this era fought to escape troubles in their native countries. For example, many Irish immigrants came to escape the **famine** caused by crop failures in Ireland. Sometimes, however, newcomers arrived in the United States only to find a new set of problems waiting for them.

These nonnatives had to find ways to survive in their new home. Numerous working-class immigrants in Chicago received aid from Jane Addams. She founded the Hull House, one of the first settlements made to make the lives of foreigners better. The Hull House offered community activities, education, work training, and other services to give newly arrived immigrants a chance at success.

Immigration Today

Today, immigrants make up a large percentage of the United States population. They come from diverse countries, such as Mexico, China, India, the Philippines, Vietnam, El Salvador, Cuba, and Korea. Numerous nonnatives arrive with advanced degrees. In many cases, children of these immigrants do better economically than their parents, and they are more likely than the average American to attend college. Immigrants have helped and continue to help our economy grow. They are among our top inventors, entrepreneurs, and job creators. They are the backbone of our country.

WordBlast

What do you think **famine** means? How does the text help you figure that out?

The Automobile

Think about this: A little more than one hundred years ago, drivers started Henry Ford's Model T with a hand crank. Today? Some cars drive themselves!

Henry Ford's Model T changed the way people saw the automobile.

Historians believe that France's Nicolas-Joseph Cugnot built the first automobile all the way back in 1769. His vehicle ran on steam, as did many that followed. In 1885, Karl Benz pioneered the gasoline-powered car. His work pushed others to continue innovating. When Ford introduced the Model T in 1908, his invention changed the face of transportation because it was inexpensive and easy to maintain. Ford turned what most saw as a luxury item into something affordable—and necessary.

Today, innovators have continued transforming the automobile. For instance, gas-powered engines produce carbon dioxide, which damages the environment over time. But gasoline is no longer the only way to power our cars, thanks to inventions such as electric cars, which run on electricity after being plugged into a power source. Hybrid cars, powered by both gas and electricity, also reduce the use of gasoline.

With the rise of electric, hybrid, and self-driving cars, the automobile has a bright and exciting future. What's next?

Self-driving cars (above) and electric cars (right) are on our roads today.

Take Action!

More to Explore

What else would you like to know about life in the young United States? Here are more questions that you can research and discuss.

How did Lewis and Clark's exploration of the West change Americans' views of their nation?

What role did transportation play in the growth of the United States?

Find out more about James Monroe. What do you think were his most significant contributions as president?

WordBlast

- What destination did Lewis and Clark **eventually** reach?
- Which **faction** did Alexander Hamilton support in the American Revolution?
- Why would a **famine** cause people to leave their country?
- What can make a road **treacherous**?

ESSENTIAL EQ QUESTION

Reflect

How were the early years of the United States transformative for the nation?

Chapter 8

THE WESTWARD EXPANSION

ESSENTIAL QUESTION EQ

What does the westward expansion reveal about the character of our nation?

Table of Contents

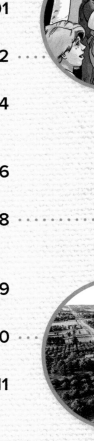

Emigrants Crossing the Plains

The trip across the plains was not an easy one. The days were long, often beginning at sunrise.

Wagon wheels were made of wood, and they often broke on rocky terrain.

Women packed food supplies such as flour, bacon, and preserved fruits and vegetables to cook the family's meals. There was always coffee, too, for the adults.

These images provide a glimpse of what life was like for pioneers crossing the plains.

- What does the top picture show about the pioneers' westward journey?
- What do you think meals along the trail were like?

(bkgd spread)olrg/Shutterstock.com, (t)Ann Ronan Pictures/Print Collector/Hulton Archive/Getty Images, (c)Pranamit/Shutterstock.com, (b spread)Kruglov_Orda/Shutterstock.com

THE CALIFORNIA TRAIL
STORY AND ART: EUREKA COMICS
OREGON TRAIL
IN THE 1850s, THE AMERICAN EMIGRANT TRAIL SYSTEM STRETCHES 3,000 MILES FROM MISSOURI TO CALIFORNIA.
CALIFORNIA TRAIL
THE CALIFORNIA TRAIL SPLITS AWAY FROM THE OREGON TRAIL IN SOUTHERN IDAHO.
IN IDAHO, TRAVELERS WRITE THEIR NAMES ON THE TOWERING FORMATIONS OF THE CITY OF ROCKS. SOME NAMES ARE STILL VISIBLE TODAY.
HEY, WHERE'S MY AXLE GREASE?
JON A GALLIHER 4.52
A. FREEMAN
D. TURNER 12.50
BEYOND IS A SERIES OF STREAMS AND RIVERS. THE SETTLERS AND THEIR ANIMALS CAN FIND THE WATER AND GRASS THEY NEED TO SURVIVE.
THEN THE TRAIL FOLLOWS THE HUMBOLDT RIVER FOR THREE HUNDRED MILES. TRAVELERS COMPLAIN ABOUT THE RIVER'S MUDDY, SMELLY WATER.
THE ANIMALS WON'T TOUCH THE RIVER WATER UNLESS WE FLAVOR IT WITH COFFEE.

THE HUMBOLDT RIVER EMPTIES INTO THE *HUMBOLDT SINK*, A GIANT SWAMP.
NEXT, THE TRAIL LEADS INTO NEVADA AND ACROSS THE FORTY MILE DESERT.
SETTLERS AND THEIR ANIMALS HAVE TO ENDURE TWO DAYS WITHOUT WATER.
THOSE WHO SURVIVE EVENTUALLY REACH THE VALLEY OF EITHER THE TRUCKEE RIVER OR THE CARSON RIVER.
THE FINAL OBSTACLE IS A STEEP 75-MILE PASSAGE THROUGH THE SIERRA NEVADA MOUNTAINS.
BETWEEN 1835 AND 1867, OVER 250,000 EMIGRANTS FOLLOW THE CALIFORNIA TRAIL TOWARD THEIR DREAMS OF A NEW LIFE.

Through Children's Eyes

by **Sandra Weber**

Young pioneers on the California Trail faced dangers and hardships, but they also had fun and saw interesting sights. "To me the journey was a 'pleasure-trip,'—so many beautiful wild flowers, such wild scenery, mountains, rocks, and streams—something new at every turn," recalled Sarah Ide, who made the trip west in 1845.

The first pioneer child to cross the Sierra Nevada Mountains into California was carried in her mother's arms. Ann Kelsey, of the Bidwell-Bartleson party of 1841, was only six months old. Five years later, thirteen-year-old Mary Murphy tried to walk across the snowy mountains, but "the snow was soft and we would almost sink to our neck." Seven-year-old Benjamin Bonney walked barefoot on the plains in 1844. Later he recalled "how we limped across the desert, for we cut the soles of our feet on the prickly pears."

Even on the trail, children did chores. They milked cows and tended livestock. In the evening, the children gathered sagebrush and buffalo chips to fuel the cooking fires. Younger members of the Stephens party shot wild ducks, geese, sage hens, antelope, and deer.

(bkgd spread)Danita Delimont/Gallo Images/Getty Images

After the work was done, "we waded the creek, made mud pies, and gathered posies," wrote Eliza Donner. Sometimes the older children would invite little children to sit behind them on their horse, "and away we would canter with the breeze playing through our hair."

Not everything was always well, however. Benjamin Bonney said that there was a good deal of sickness at Fort Sutter and "a large number of natives died as well as some of the emigrants, mainly children." Another danger was the possibility of falling off a wagon and getting run over by its wheels.

Despite some horrible situations, the children found moments of delight. Little girls "used to fill the pretty porcelain tea-cups with freshly fallen snow, daintily dip it out with teaspoons and eat it, playing it was custard." Patty Reed held onto a wooden doll and a lock of her grandmother's hair to remind her of happier times.

When they finally reached California, pioneers found good weather and food. "The ground was covered with fine green grass and there was a very fat beef hanging from the branch of an oak tree," wrote John Breen, age fifteen. "The birds were singing . . . and the journey was over."

Travelers gathered together at night to eat, fill their water barrels, and rest for the next day.

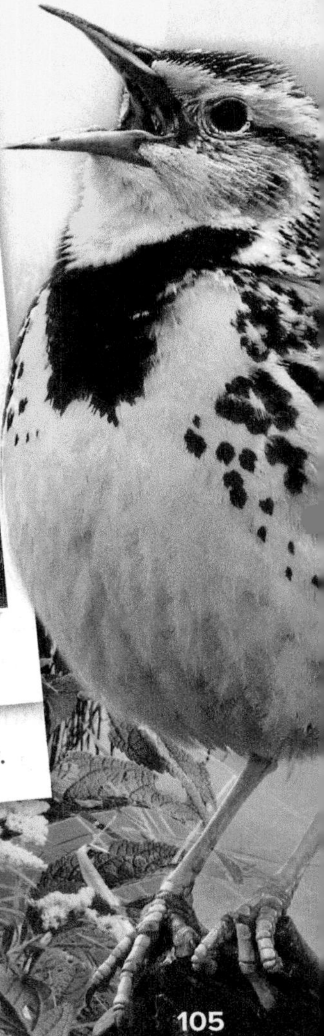

PERSPECTIVES

THE WORDS OF CHIEF JOSEPH

Chief Joseph was a leader of the Nez Perce.

The Nez Perce meet with an employee of the Union Pacific Railway.

Imagine this: A group of strangers comes into your home. You never invited them inside, but you treat them kindly nonetheless. The strangers seem grateful at first. Then things start to change. Before you know it, the strangers have taken over and force you to leave your home forever.

Countless Native Americans lost a great deal because of the American settlers. While moving west offered settlers new opportunities, Native Americans suffered dreadful losses.

Chief Joseph was a leader of the Nez Perce. In an article published in 1879, he **recounted** the history of his tribe as settlers moved into Nez Perce lands in the Pacific Northwest.

(bkgd spread)Steve Terrill/Corbis Documentary/Getty Images, (l) Buyenlarge/Archive Photos/Getty Images, (tr)Carleton E. Watkins/ Stringer/Hulton Archive/Getty Images, (br)Grosvenor Prints/ Chronicle/Alamy Stock Photo

PRIMARY SOURCE

Kind Beginnings

The first white men of your people who came to our country were named Lewis and Clark. . . . They talked straight, and our people gave them a great feast, as a proof that their hearts were friendly. These men . . . made presents to our chiefs and our people made presents to them. . . . All the Nez Perces made friends with Lewis and Clark, and agreed to let them pass through their country, and never to make war on white men. This promise the Nez Perces have never broken.

Growing Concerns

When my father was a young man there came to our country a white man . . . . At first, he did not say anything about white men wanting to settle on our lands. Nothing was said about that until about twenty winters ago, when a number of white people came into our country and built houses and made farms. At first our people made no complaint. They thought there was room enough for all to live in peace. . . . But we soon found that the white men . . . were greedy to possess everything the Indian had.

Betrayed

For a short time we lived quietly. But this could not last. White men had found gold in the mountains. . . . They stole a great many horses from us, and we could not get them back because we were Indians. . . . They drove off a great many of our cattle. Some white men branded our young cattle so they could claim them. We had no friend who would plead our cause before the law councils. It seemed to me that some of the white men in Wallowa were doing these things on purpose to get up a war. They knew that we were not strong enough to fight them. I labored hard to avoid trouble and bloodshed. We gave up some of our country to the white men, thinking that then we could have peace. We were mistaken. . . . We could have avenged our wrongs many times, but we did not. . . . The Nez Perces wished to live in peace.

WordBlast

Recounted means "told a story or described events." What story does Chief Joseph recount in the article?

TEXT: Chief Young Joseph. "An Indian's Views of Indian Affairs." The North American Review 128, no. 269 (April 1879): 412-434; PHOTO: mariait/Shutterstock.com

Gold Rush Writers

The California Gold Rush gave American authors something new to write about. Bret Harte came to California in 1854. He worked briefly as a schoolteacher and then a miner before turning to writing. In one of his best-known tales, "The Luck of Roaring Camp," Harte told about an unusual event in mining life:

> "Deaths were by no means uncommon in Roaring Camp, but a birth was a new thing. . . . Above the swaying and moaning of the pines, the swift rush of the river, and the crackling of the fire, rose a sharp, . . . cry, . . . unlike anything heard before in the camp. The pines stopped moaning, the river ceased to rush, and the fire to crackle. It seemed as if Nature had stopped to listen too."

Samuel Clemens
(Mark Twain)

Another famous American author, Samuel Clemens, came to California in 1864 after failing at silver mining in Nevada. Gold mining proved just as **fruitless**, so he picked up the pen. Writing under the pen name Mark Twain, he explored the humorous side of mining life in his book *Roughing It.*

> "The honest miner raked from a hundred to a thousand dollars out of his claim a day, and what with the gambling dens and the other entertainments, he hadn't a cent the next morning, if he had any sort of luck."

The Gold Rush resulted not only in great wealth but also in great American literature. It brought California and the colorful miners to the attention of a worldwide audience.

Bret Harte

WordBlast

What word in the text about Samuel Clemens means the same as **fruitless**? Use a dictionary to confirm your answer.

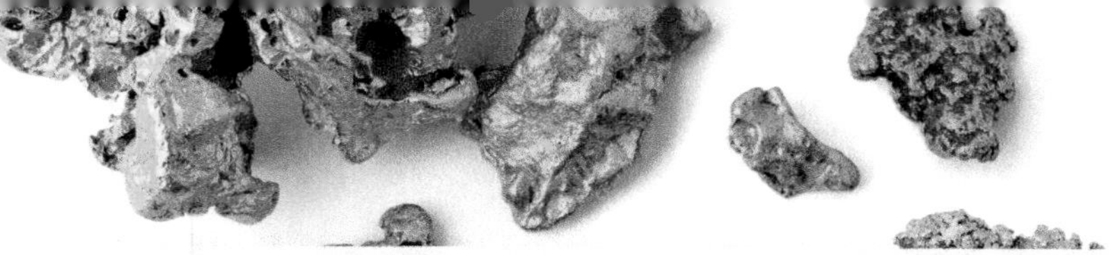

from "The Shirley Letters from California Mines in 1851-52"

by Dame Shirley

Mrs. Louise Amelia Knapp Smith Clappe went west with her husband. Between 1851 and 1852, Dame Shirley (her pen name) wrote twenty-three letters to her sister in Massachusetts from the California mines. The letters were later published in a literary magazine called Pioneer. *The letters are a unique, firsthand look at life in two gold mining camps.*

Nothing of importance has happened since I last wrote you, except that I have become a *mineress,* that is, if the having washed a pan of dirt with my own hands, and procured therefrom three dollars and twenty-five cents in gold-dust, . . . will entitle me to the name. I can truly say . . . that I am sorry I learned the trade, for I wet my feet, . . . got an awful headache, took cold, and lost a valuable breastpin, in this my labor of love. After such **melancholy** self-sacrifice on my part, I trust you will duly prize my gift. I can assure you that it is the last golden handiwork you will ever receive from Dame Shirley.

. . . I succeeded, after much awkward maneuvering on my own part, and considerable assistance from . . . an experienced miner, in gathering together the above-specified sum. All the diggers . . . say that it is an excellent "prospect," even to come from the bed-rock, where, naturally, the richest dirt is found. To be sure, there are, now and then, "lucky strikes," . . . where a person took out of a single basinful of soil two hundred and fifty-six dollars. But such luck is as rare as the winning of a hundred-thousand-dollar prize in a lottery. We are acquainted with many here whose gains have *never* amounted to much more than wages, that is, from six to eight dollars a day. And a claim which yields a man a steady income of ten dollars *per diem* is considered as very valuable.

WordBlast

Melancholy means "sad." According to the text, what events made Dame Shirley melancholy?

TEXT: Dame Shirley to her sister, 25 November 1851. In The Shirley Letters from California Mines in 1851-52, ed. Thomas C. Russell, no. 10. San Francisco: Thomas C. Russell Private Press, 1922. PHOTO: (t)Gilles Paire/Shutterstock.com, (tr)Library of Congress Prints and Photographs Division [LC-USZC2-1755], (b spread)Doug Meek/Corbis Documentary/Getty Images

Citizenship

Cherokee Chief

WILMA MANKILLER

Wilma Mankiller was a strong voice for social justice, Native Americans, and women.

Wilma Mankiller was a great leader of the Cherokee people. "Mankiller" was a Cherokee name of respect for warriors who guarded their villages. Wilma, whose father was a full-blooded Cherokee, took pride in her name. Born in 1945, she grew up on tribal lands in Oklahoma. Her family moved to San Francisco hoping for new opportunities. However, they experienced poverty and unemployment.

In the 1960s, Native Americans took over a closed federal prison, Alcatraz, in San Francisco. Wilma visited these activists and became inspired to do more to help her people. She took college courses and coordinated Native American programs for public schools.

Mankiller soon moved back to Oklahoma. To help people with basic needs—clean water and decent housing—she created the Community Development Department for the Cherokee Nation. In 1983, she became Deputy Chief of the Cherokee Nation. When the chief left to lead another agency, Mankiller became chief in 1987. A woman had never held this position, but she demonstrated commitment, strength, and ability. She was re-elected in 1991.

Mankiller helped the Cherokee community make great advances in health, education, employment, and housing. In 1998, President Clinton awarded her the Medal of Freedom, America's highest **civilian** honor. She died in 2010.

WordBlast

The word *civil* refers to the ordinary people in a community. How does that help you know the meaning of **civilian**? Use a dictionary to verify the meaning.

Take Action!

More to Explore

What did you read that you would like to know more about? Here are more questions that you can research and discuss.

How did the emigrants prepare to permanently leave their homes in the East?

What artifacts have been found from the time of the westward expansion? What do they reveal about life on the trail?

How did Chief Joseph try to help his people, the Nez Perce?

WordBlast

- Who is a high-ranking **civilian** in your community?
- Give an example of a **fruitless** effort in sports, politics, or popular culture.
- What experiences might have given pioneers feelings of **melancholy**?
- **Recount** what you did yesterday in school.

ESSENTIAL EQ QUESTION

Reflect

What does the westward expansion reveal about the character of our nation?

What Do I Say?

Here are some ways you can talk with a partner or a small group.

Remember to . . .

Ask questions that add to the conversation.

- Why do you think the author said this?
- Why do you think that? Tell me more.
- I'm confused by . . . .

LWA/Dann Tardif/Blend Images/Getty Images

Connect ideas to other texts or situations.

- This reminds me of what we learned in . . . .
- This is a lot like . . . .
- This makes me think about . . . .

Help your partner explain more.

- Do you mean that . . . ?
- Can you explain that?
- Can you give me more examples?

Talk about what your partner said earlier.

- What you said made me think about . . . .
- I'd like to add to what you just said.
- I want to go back to what you said before.

Challenge an idea.

- Where in the text did you find that evidence?
- Show me where the author says that.
- How do you know that?

Clear up misunderstandings.

- Okay, so what you're saying is . . . .
- What do you mean by . . . ?
- I'm not sure I know what you mean. Can you explain?

Disagree politely.

- I hear what you're saying. I also think that . . . .
- I'm not so sure. Maybe . . . .
- I see it differently.

Support your ideas with examples.

- In the text it says that . . . .
- For example . . . .
- The reason I think this is because . . . .

WordBlast

A

allegiance
loyalty to a country or ruler

altitude
the height of something

B

barter
to exchange goods or services without using money

C

circumnavigate
to sail all the way around the world

civilian
a person who is an ordinary citizen, not a member of the military or police force

clearing
a small area in the middle of a forest where there are no trees

commemorate
to observe with a celebration or ceremony

cultivate
to till or prepare the soil

E

eloquence
impressive or persuasive speaking skills

engrave
to cut words into stone or wood

eventually
at a later time, in the end

excavate
to dig up in an orderly way

exterminate
to kill off completely

F

faction
a group within a larger group that has different ideas from the people in the larger group

famine
a shortage of food

feasible
possible to carry out

ferocity
the state of being violent, cruel, or severe

fruitless
failing to achieve what was wanted

G

generation
all the people who are born and live around the same time period

I

intercept
to stop someone or something from reaching its destination

J

jeopardy
the state of being in danger

M

melancholy
feeling sad

microbe
a tiny organism that can cause disease

N

network
a system of people who work together

P

persevere
to continue through difficult times

R

ratify
to approve legally

recount
to tell a story or describe events

retaliation
the act of doing something bad to someone who has hurt you

revolutionary
a person who supports a major change—typically the removal and replacement of a government

T

terrain
a type of land

treacherous
full of danger or treachery